St Austell County Grammar Schools

1908-75

"BY THE SMELL OF THE BREWERY

AND

WITH THE VIEW OVER THE BAY"

BY
MARY ABBOTT
WITH RESEARCHER MARIE GURNETT

RRP £11.95 • ISBN No: 0-9549005-5-3
Published by: Blue Hills Publishing Web: www.bluehillspublishing.co.uk
Design: Louise Hillier Designs • Tel: 01872 554490 E-mail: loo@zoom.co.uk

CONTENTS

ACKNOWLEDGEMENTS

Much archive material from the School in its various forms was accumulated over the years, largely by Miss Margaret Husband, and carefully preserved. When I retired from what was then St Austell College in 1999, Richard Turner, a colleague and an Old Boy (1956-63), suggested I make use of this material and compile a history of the School. An Old Girl Marie Gurnett (Bennetto 1955-62) agreed to help me.

We have used minutes of Governors' Meetings from 1908, supplementing our material with that at the County Record Office in Truro. As well as the Log Books from 1926, we were able to gain access to virtually all of the Magazines, again plugging the gaps with very kind loans from old students as well as St Austell County Library and the Cornish Studies Library at Redruth. Roger Smith and Tony Lake of the History Department of Poltair School, gave us the results of a survey they had carried out with their pupils in the 1990s, which questioned former students on their memories. These were most valuable. Molly Richards (Light 1942-7) opened many doors for us for the 1930s and 1940s, and without her support we should have found it extremely difficult to access important memories of that period. Many an Old Student Reunion, mostly of girls it has to be said, has welcomed us and provided us with the essentially human, anecdotal memories which are so important, as well as the more officially factual material. Some of you responded to my plea in the Cornish Guardian in 2005, giving even more insight into pupil perceptions. The School was fortunate to inherit Miss Parry's many photographs, and more precious memorabilia and photographs have been entrusted to us by former students and their families and we are hugely grateful to all those who have contributed. Indeed, although there are unfortunate gaps, we have a vast number of photographs which has made selection extremely difficult and we hope we have not caused offence by omission. We have included names where known and appropriate, but particularly with the early photographs this has not always been possible.

There has also been a dedicated band of friends who were prepared to give their time to read this through and help to eliminate glaring errors and discrepancies.

Without this support and encouragement we suspect that we may have been defeated in what became a daunting, if very interesting, exercise.

Thank you one and all.

Mary Abbott

Marie Gurnett

1. LAYING THE FOUNDATIONS

The original building 1908

The passing of the Balfour Education Act of 1902 placed the responsibility of providing state secondary education on the local education authorities. While there was a Grammar School in Fowey of 17th century foundation, there was nothing in the St Austell district. In the provision of elementary education St Austell had been in the forefront nationally, the St Austell Board having established one of the first Board Schools at Mount Charles, in 1872, following Forster's Education Act of 1870. Soon there was a will both locally and in the County Education Committee, that the good work in providing elementary education should be built upon by establishing a County Secondary School.

With great ceremony foundation stones were laid in 1906 for a school for 200 pupils from the district, which would provide the best possible secondary education. Building on the work of the St Austell Pupil Teachers' Centre, which had opened in the summer of 1905, it aimed not only to produce pupil teachers but also to give local children the best opportunities to compete in the industrial world as well as to contribute positively to the formation of character. The School was to cost £5,000 to build with a further £650 for the playing field behind. It would now be possible for able children to proceed from their local elementary schools to a more advanced education. For the first time, children from families with limited means could enjoy such education with scholarships from the County, and children from more substantial families would no longer have to be sent away, probably out of County, to gain their education.

St Austell County Secondary School opened in September 1908 with 101 pupils, from the age of 8 to 18, both fee paying and scholarship. Fees were 6 guineas (£6.6/-) per year with a further subscription to the Games Fund of 2/6d per term; the County, of course, paying the latter for free scholars. From the first School Magazine, of the winter of 1908, first day experiences of the pupils include reports that there was a carriage drive for bicycles paved with sand and the fact that all were impressed with the views from the upper windows, something which all future pupils and staff have appreciated. Clearly, the use of bicycles was critical, with no public transport as such, and in August 1908, the Governors authorised the building of a Bicycle Shed for £10. There is some evidence that pupils lodged in St Austell during the week, going home at the weekend – an arrangement which Anne Treneer describes in her renowned autobiographical trilogy *School House in the Wind*, Gorran being too far for daily excursions in pony and trap.

The Headmaster was Mr WD Raynor and Senior Mistress, Miss M Passmore, both of whom had held similar positions in the Pupil Teachers' Centre (PTC). There were five further members of staff, two from the PTC, and the curriculum covered the basic subjects of English, Mathematics, Science, French, History, Geography and Latin, with a visiting Art teacher. By 1909 there was also a Woodwork teacher and visiting instrumental Music teacher, while some singing lessons were given by existing members of staff. Salaries of the full time staff ranged from £100 per year to £130 with £200 for the Headmaster, while the caretaker earned £40. From the outset school dinners were provided at a cost of 2/- per week, which were an extension of the PTC arrangements. This gained the full support of the Governors in November 1909, when they considered this provision to be a great inducement to children living outside the town, to attend St Austell rather than Fowey. Kitchen equipment, however, was a permanent subject for discussion among the Governors as there was never enough money to provide what it was felt was needed. Indeed a sub-committee of the lady Governors, together with Miss Passmore, was appointed to make recommendations. In 1909 it was thought that the County should be made aware of the fact that the children were eating their meals in the same room as the cooking was done. There was a suggestion that a screen, perhaps 'a clothes horse covered in serge', should be used as a divider.

Public examinations were taken from the beginning. The first were the Preliminary Certificate Examinations which had been taken in the PTC, with a number of pupils taking Cambridge Local Examinations in 1909, one of whom was Anne Treneer. The two series of examinations continued side by side until 1912 when, in line with other County Schools, the Preliminary Certificate Examination was discarded in favour of the Oxford or Cambridge Locals.

The award of prizes for good work was begun at the end of 1909 with 31 pupils receiving form and subject prizes amounting to £7.0/9d, ranging from 2/6d for the youngest to 6/3d for the most senior.

The PTC had requested playing fields in 1906 but it was not until late 1908 that the playing fields on the School site could begin to be used for football and hockey. The goal posts cost 2 guineas and were only half painted because they ran out of paint! The town cricket field, then just down the road, was hired for £3.10/- per season, with tennis being played on the 'playfields', as they were called. Although there are reports of initial cutting and rolling, there were difficulties about keeping the playing fields in an appropriate condition and there was much discussion in Governors' Meetings as to when Mr Kelly should 'depasture his sheep on the playfield'.

From that time boys regularly played football matches against local teams and the other County Schools, sometimes with younger masters in the team! The 1909 season was very successful as the beginning of a long poem in the School Magazine illustrates:

St Austell County School can boast a football team A1,
To which is due all praise for laurels fairly won;
Against no team they falter, no side they think too strong,
And sound in wind and limb, no game they think too long.

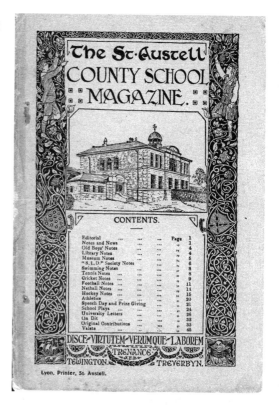

The hockey did not begin so auspiciously and this was attributed to the girls' lack of stamina! The boys' football jerseys were red and gold, 'Aston Villa style', the girls' hockey uniform is not recorded although their corner flags were yellow and black. Cricket flourished during the summer months with the girls, too, raising a team. In summer 1909 there were 42 members of the tennis club but other problems were encountered as the magazine of 1909 reports: 'We have found our exposed situation makes the wind a factor in outdoor badminton which renders the game impossible'!

From 1910 the Headmaster was able to invite guest speakers to the School to supplement the curriculum, and a variety of lectures, some with musical accompaniment, became a permanent feature of the life of the School. The musical activities which were later to become such an important part of the extra curricular tradition of the School, began in December 1910 with a concert given by the choir in the Public Rooms, conducted by Mr Cattle who also taught Geography. Dramatic performances, too, began in February 1909 and they included French and Latin plays as well as scenes from Shakespeare. These were produced by Miss Passmore (English, History and Latin), Miss Thomas (French) and Mr Lodge (Mathematics and Physics).

There was an embryonic Library begun by Miss Passmore, which consisted of 135 books and a book case, and in 1908 the County made a grant of £7.10/- which was to be match funded by books raised by the School.

The Governors were continually preoccupied with problems with the water supply which was, initially, provided by the Urban District Council. In 1908 it was deemed to be sufficient for 'ordinary purposes', which were not specified but were probably few, but totally inadequate in the event of fire. It was fortunate that none occurred in the early days, especially as a request to the County in 1908 for a Minimax fire extinguisher was constantly referred back, until finally rejected in 1914. Special discounting arrangements were made with the St Austell Gas Company, presumably for lighting and laboratory purposes, while the heating must have been some sort of central heating as there are records of tenders for coal, coke and anthracite.

It was from these beginnings that there sprang a history of some 67 years, incorporating the separate Girls' and Boys' County Grammar Schools of the 1930s, '40s and '50s, and the final flourishing of the Mixed Grammar School in the 1960s.

2. THE EARLY YEARS

In spite of all the fine words spoken in 1906, the School did not enjoy a trouble free start. There was opposition, both in the town and among members of the governing body, to mixed secondary education. It was thought that it was not seemly that children should be taught in mixed classes and that the educational needs of growing boys and girls were considered to be completely different.

Indeed, the minutes of the Governors' Meetings of 1909 recount a long running complaint by a local clergyman concerning the education which his daughter was, or was not receiving. Lack of discipline, boys and girls being allowed 'to mingle together', and methods of teaching drawing were among the criticisms cited. This was resolved only by the withdrawal of the girl from the School. Then there was the 'scandalous' disciplinary case, in 1910, when a parent claimed that a boy had behaved in a lewd manner in front of his daughter, while at school. Again there was a long running saga. The boy himself was 12½, two years older than the next boy in his form the age range of which was 8¾ to 12½ which must, of itself, have created other problems besides this one. The origin of the incident appears to have been the studying of an, at that time, well known children's poem, 'Where did you come from, baby dear?' The boy was, initially, suspended but reinstated after the LEA (Local Education Authority) became involved. It is poignant that the boy's name later appears on the board commemorating those Old Boys who had lost their lives in the First World War.

These two blows were difficult for the new School and were compounded by a poor Inspection Report. Mr Raynor resigned when confronted with charges of lack of discipline and poor organisation of his staff.

Numbers of pupils did not rise, in fact there were some serious fluctuations. In 1913 they had fallen to 77 and three teachers were given ½ term's notice – and there were exactly the same number on roll in May 1915 as there had been at the opening, 101. In July 1912 the question why the School was not attracting sufficient numbers was again asked by the Governors. One of the inevitable answers was that the School was mixed.

Mr A Jenkinson, a much sterner disciplinarian than his predecessor, became the second Headmaster in 1910. Staff numbers had swelled to ten, all were graduates of British universities, apart from those teaching practical subjects. A visiting Cookery teacher was paid 3/- per hour plus travelling expenses, as long as there was a class of a minimum of twelve girls. Cooking utensils were to be shared with the School Kitchen which occasionally led to some disharmony! A 'military man' was appointed to teach the boys drill but the request for a French/German 'assistante' was rejected by the Board of Education. So, the curriculum was beginning to expand. Evening classes became a feature, usually Art, Agriculture and Woodwork, together with the provision of facilities for a special class for Engineering subjects for the Clay District, under the auspices of the Technical Instruction Scheme. Teaching aids were few and far between, although, in 1911, permission was given to hire 350 lantern slides for 1 guinea.

For the pupils themselves it cannot always have been easy. There is mention in the early Magazines of the problems associated with the crossing gates at the bottom of Trevarthian Road which were frequently shut for shunting – the footbridge was not built until 1931. Another poem in a Magazine bewails:

In minutes five the bell will ring,
But hindered, I, by cruel fate:
It is no Fury bars the way,
Only a level crossing gate.

Ne'er have I yet been late for school,
My anger scarce can I express:
What can it be that hinders now?
It comes! Behold! A goods express!

In the same Magazine there is a (half serious) request that the UDC (Urban District Council) provide stilts to be picked up at the crossing gates, 'as the road between the crossing and the school is generally a river of mud'. Many, of course, came from much farther afield and there is reference, in 1910, to the irregular attendance of a Free Scholar, one Winifred Watts. She cycled the nine miles each way from Whitemoor and inclement weather often affected her journeys!

There was some concern about the standards the children were reaching and, in May 1911, permission was asked from the County to refuse admission to those who could not read or write! The following year the Headmaster examined the whole school in all subjects and found that grammar was very defective.

But it was not all doom and gloom. The first Speech Day was held in July 1910, when the prizes were presented by Sir Arthur Quiller Couch, or 'Q' as he was known, who encouraged 'the more important people' present, the pupils, to set the tone of the new school. The County Council had put up that school and the boys and girls had to build it with their lives, and he asked them to be worthy of it.

Reading prizes were also awarded, two to those over fifteen and two under fifteen. There were so many entrants the first year, 1911, that preliminary trials had to be held the previous day. A prefect system was introduced in 1910, with nine being appointed, and, in 1911, a reading stand for morning prayers was purchased for them, for 15/-. By 1914 there were two Houses, Treverbyn, which won the House Shield in 1915, and Tewington. Trenance was created in 1916 when numbers had risen to 155.

The years before the First World War saw a gradual development of the extra-curricular activities and, perhaps, the heart of the School. Games flourished, especially football with the girls' hockey becoming more prominent – presumably the girls were developing their stamina! Cricket for both girls and boys was well established and in 1911 the first annual Sports Day was held on the town football ground. In March of the same year there is an amusing account of a paper chase which went through Tregonissey and Carclaze, up to the black-smith's shop at the top of the hill, down to the Bodmin Road, through Trethowal and past the Ruddlemoor Clay Works until the 'hares', who were resting, were caught by the 'hounds'. It is a tale of much puffing and panting, to say nothing of deception by various children and locals who gave misleading information! A Debating Society

was going strong by 1913 and the Music continued to flourish with the choir winning the County Vintner Shield on the first occasion that it was open to mixed schools. Although Miss Passmore left in 1913, the seeds had been sown for regular dramatic performances. The girls formed the Fairy Godmother Club which sent dolls and clothes to missions and orphanages. In December 1910 separate Old Boys' and Old Girls' Associations were formed but, as subsequently, neither really took off, apart from operating as a dramatic society in the 1930s and '40s.

There was the odd unexpected holiday as in June 1909 when the School closed for the visit to the town of the Prince and Princess of Wales, and again in May 1911 for the Coronation of George V. But the request, in December 1910, that the School should close for Feast Week in 1911 was rejected.

Initially the outbreak of the First World War in August 1914 passed without mention in the Governors' Minutes, presumably because this 'Mince Pie War' would be over by Christmas, with no anticipation of the horrors which were to follow. However, there were soon obvious effects on the personnel of the School. Late in 1914 a Belgian refugee, Emil Goethals, became a pupil, although he did not stay long. As the Magazine of the winter of 1915 describes: 'We had to lose our popular Belgian scholar who has gone to France with the Belgian army. He was a great loss, especially to our football team, but he went, (entirely on his own initiative), to do his duty to his King and country.' Towards the end of the War there were further Belgian refugees, all of whom were exempt from the payment of fees. In February 1915 the Headmaster and another member of staff, Mr Mellers, joined up and went to War. The Magazine of the summer of 1915 reports that Mr Mellers was wounded in France, and after the War he took up another appointment and did not return to St Austell. Mr Lodge became acting Headmaster for the duration of the War. Following a request to the Governors, at least one family, from Bugle, had the fees of their son remitted, when SM Jacob's father went to War and could no longer pay the fees.

By the end of 1915 the desirability of starting gardening classes for boys and girls was aired and the next summer, Mr Lodge turned some waste ground on the School site into a garden. He asked members of the School to bring contributions to stock it. By October 1917, it had produced a welcome ½ ton of potatoes for school dinners, together with useful cabbages and greens. Rather more drastically, in 1915 it was decreed that no young man should be admitted to Evening Classes in Agriculture unless he could prove his ineligibility for Service – a reflection, no doubt, of the prevailing mood of the time.

A Rifle Club was formed in the School in 1914, and in 1915 a School Cadet Corps by the Rev Lawson, who subsequently was called to the front as a chaplain. It had three sections: Ambulance, Cyclist and Signalling and it was from this that the School Signalling Corps developed during the following year, with instruction in more specific signalling techniques combined with two long route marches during half term and at the end of the summer term. In the autumn of 1916, £3.12/- was raised for the Daily News and Daily Telegraph Fund to send Christmas puddings to soldiers, and, in 1917, a War Savings Association was formed.

Economies had to be made and, in December 1915, no prizes were given, the money going to a charity of the pupils' choice, which is not recorded. In May 1918 fuel supplies were so short and erratic that the Governors authorised the purchase of coal and anthracite during the summer months. There was also a real shortage of food resulting, in February 1918, in the strictest of economies in the School Kitchen. There was to be a meatless day each week and the products of the School garden proved to be invaluable. In the autumn of 1917 the School responded to a Board of Education initiative when Mr Lodge and Miss Thomas took a large squad of boys and girls to Pentewan woods and collected a large sack full of chestnuts. The collection of these conkers was encouraged because 'this collection is invaluable war work and is very urgent' (Ministry of Supply). Apparently there was a secret plan to substitute conkers for maize, the import of which had become very difficult because of shipping blockades. The starch extracted was used in the making of acetone which was a key ingredient in the manufacture of cordite. St Austell's collection

Some Staff and Prefects 1918: **Back row:** *Henry Dyer, Ivy Best, Ray Richards, H Mitchell, Leslie Sleep, J Popplewell, Stewart Sweet, Helen Whetter, Lionel Pell(?)* **Front row:** *???, Mr Gornall, Miss Blank, Mr Lodge (acting headmaster), Miss Twigg (?) (Senior Mistress), ???, Miss Parry*

Football Team 1918-19

would probably have been transported to Poole but this was not entirely satisfactory as, apparently, logistical problems left piles of rotting conkers on railway stations!

Sad news of Old Boys who were casualties in the War began to come through and, while, surprisingly, there is no reference to them in the Governors' Minutes, the Magazines gave accounts of their deaths. In total the number was comparatively small, bearing in mind the long lists of names on War Memorials up and down the country, and in St Austell Parish Church yard itself. But the School had been in existence for such a short time that there were not many Old Boys anyway. The School Magazine of 1920 lists 103 Old Boys, in total, who served during the course of the War, in a wide variety of regiments and occupations.

The life of the School continued to develop in spite of the War. There was a slight change of emphasis in the curriculum with the County encouraging domestic subjects – Needlework had been taught since 1912 and there was the occasional substitution of Laundry for Cooking for the girls. By 1918, the County was also suggesting the teaching of commercial subjects. This followed the School's decision to allow some pupils, from

April 1914, to take Book-keeping and Shorthand instead of Latin. There was a worrying period, however, between 1915 and 1918, when it proved to be impossible to recruit a Science teacher to replace Mr Metters. External speakers continued to visit – Mr Cardell Williams, the County Bee Expert, being particularly effective.

Pupil numbers began to rise quite spectacularly. From 101 in May 1915 they had risen to 180 (98 boys and 82 girls) in October 1917. However attendance was affected in 1916 by a prolonged outbreak of measles, with staff as well as pupils suffering. Examination results impressed the Governors throughout the War, with praise given for both Oxford and Cambridge Locals, but no details were recorded.

Extra curricular activities continued to flourish. On the sports front the football team was beginning to express itself. In 1916, it played 21 matches, winning fifteen, drawing five and losing one, and in the following year it won the East Division League. There were now two girls' hockey teams with the 1st X1 making impressive journeys to play their matches. For instance, the Magazine of the autumn of 1917 gives the following account: 'The team cycled to Fowey in ideal hockey weath-

Hockey XI 1915: Miss Blank, Ruth Lomer, Amy Sarah, Hilda Whetter, Hilda Mitchell, Hilda, Lyndon (Sec), Erna Cook; Vera Morshead, Ivy Best (Capt), Marion Yelland; ????, Violet Lean, Julia Best

er, but they felt far from fresh at the commencement of their match…(Won 4-1)…After being entertained at the Grammar School, we started on our homeward ride. Having proved on our last visit that it was unwise to light up (bicycle lamps) on the top of the hill, we performed this ceremony in a corner of Fore Street. We reached St Austell at about 7.30pm, having been very fortunate in the matter of punctures and having comparatively little trouble with our lamps.' In June 1915, the fourth annual Sports Day was held but, as for the duration of the War, no prizes were presented. In 1917 the newly appointed Miss Parry introduced netball although it was not until 1919 that matches were played against other schools. She also began swimming classes in the summer, taking senior girls to Porthpean on Monday afternoons, instead of drill. Cricket, too, flourished, although by 1918 Miss Blank was deputising for the Games Master and umpired every match for both boys and girls.

The Debating Society adopted strict new rules for members. From 1917 they would be fined 2d if they failed to speak during the course of a debate. Staff were active members, too, and in October 1917 the motion: 'That a Channel Tunnel should be constructed' was successful, just, by 18-17. Sometimes it adopted a lighter format and in February 1919 they held a Mock Trial: 'That Samuel Clyma did, during the last lesson on Wednesday morning, October 9th 1918, unlawfully appropriate the ball used by the girls in a game of netball, and was mainly instrumental in using the aforesaid ball in the game of football'. The Magazine does not record the result but Samuel Clyma certainly lived to tell the tale!

Drama productions appear to have been concentrated into end of term celebrations combined with certificate presentations. These included, in December 1915, a patriotic pageant *Britannia's Reception*, and Goldsmith's *She Stoops to Conquer*

Above: *Netball Team 1919 with Miss Parry* **Below:** *We are not convinced that this is an early County School production but it was in the School archives. It is a splendid period piece.*

in 1916. On each occasion these were supported by musical pieces, and the choirs also continued competing in County Competitions. In 1918, Miss Parry's long reign over successful choirs began with the Mixed Choir winning the Vintner Shield and a Shield presented by Messrs John Lovering, the Boys' Choir failing by only 4% to win the Petherick Shield.

In 1918, Miss Blank introduced a Literary Society whose first meeting considered Sir Walter Scott, and the second, Lord Tennyson.

In April 1914, the Clerk to the Governors reported that he had been in communication with the GWR Co concerning cheap Road Motor fares for pupils in the St Austell district and it appears that by 1915 there was an embryonic public transport system over medium distances. Roydon Radcliffe from St Dennis was given permission by the Governors to leave and join Newquay County School because of the 'dislocation of the Motor Service between St Dennis and St Austell'. What a blessing such a service would have been for Winifred Watts!

Difficulties were encountered in establishing the provision of School dinners. In July 1913 there were only twenty pupils taking meals with the result that the operation did not pay. The Cook left and the new Senior Mistress, Miss Lomas, took charge of the dining arrangements in February 1914 – a task which was to continue to be the responsibility of Senior Mistresses. Her immediate suggestion was that the Cook's wages should be reduced from 12/6d to 10/- per week as long as the numbers remained low. But a visit by lady Governors in November noted that the cooking range was not satisfactory. In February 1915 it still had not been fixed, the situation being compounded by the fact that the gas stove also was not working. At that stage the County agreed to ensure that both were in working order. The result was that by November 1916, things had improved so much that the kitchen could no longer cope with the Cookery classes as well! The Board of Education consequently gave permission for Cookery lessons to be at the St Austell Centre at West Hill. The charge for meals was 2/2d per week, with 1d per day if this was not paid. This resulted in a father complaining that the meals were too expensive. The Headmaster had written to parents, in 1911, saying that children must take

School meals unless they could go home or eat at the home of a friend.

Physical conditions in the School were a cause of some concern by the Governors. In 1914, suggestions and plans for equipment to dry pupils' clothes were rejected by the County, following lengthy negotiations. There was, however, better news about First Aid equipment which was granted in 1914. In 1913 the heating apparatus was not capable of heating the upper rooms, but there was no improvement during the course of the War. The UDC water supply was still not satisfactory. The pressure was not great enough to supply the premises properly and the water was often discoloured, resulting in frequent negotiations with the UDC concerning the payment of dues. Overtures were begun with RDC (Rural District Council) which was considered to provide a more effective service. During the War there were no further moves on the request initially made to the County in 1912, for a 'gymnasium' which would also incorporate an Assembly Hall and a Dining Hall. At first the request had met local opposition because of the burden on the rates for such a small number of pupils.

There is no formal record of what the pupils did when they left. Certainly a number of them, inevitably, progressed to Teacher Training Colleges with Borough Road, in London, being popular, while Anne Treneer and others went to the Diocesan College in Truro. St Luke's College at Exeter was a favourite venue and the new Royal Albert Memorial College, much later to become Exeter University, also was becoming an obvious destination for those wanting a university education not too far from home. There is no information at all as to how these 'pioneers' were funded – one can only assume that their families paid, although there were a few County University Scholarships. Many others joined their family business. Indeed most must have remained and worked locally, although there is a stirring account of two brothers who became 'apprentices on ships', presumably having joined the Merchant Navy.

In April 1919, Mr Jenkinson returned from the War to resume his duties and the School continued its slow but steady progress. Pupil numbers rose to over 200 in 1919 and by September 1920 stood at 230, with equal numbers of boys and girls. Increased numbers required extra staff and

Prefects with, we think, the new Senior Mistress Miss Griffiths 1919

full time members rose to twelve. Numbers in the VIth Form stood at eight and a new Senior Mistress, Miss Griffiths, organised picnics for them, which must have provided welcome interludes. The sports teams continued to do reasonably well and the Choir continued to win the County Vintner Shield. By 1921 a party of folk dancers went to the First Cornwall Folk Dance Festival in Penzance, starting another tradition which was to last well beyond the Second World War. Speech Days were followed by dramatic performances in the Public Rooms – in 1921 it was *Twelfth Night*.

The Dining Room, known later as the 'Old Kitchen', was provided with a lift, operated manually by prefects, to take food to the upper floor, but there were continual problems concerning the accommodation and equipment, with constant requests for more money to be spent. The Library continued to expand with the County giving an annual grant – in 1921 of £7.10/-. An innovation was the provision of 41 books and 36 magazines, in 1918, for a Wet Dinner Hour Library. The health of the pupils received attention in May 1920, when medical examinations were to be

extended to secondary children, as in elementary schools – but girls must be seen by a lady doctor!

One of Mr Jenkinson's last major contribution, beyond the normal running of the school, was the organisation and dedication of the memorial to those boys who had been killed during the First World War. There had been much difficulty in raising the money for the Memorial Window and the plaque commemorating the nine Old Boys, indeed the fund was still £60 short, but an impressive ceremony was held on October 21st 1921. Mr JC Williams, the Lord Lieutenant, unveiled the window with buglers of the Duke of Cornwall Light Infantry, from the Bodmin Depot, sounding the Last Post and Reveille while wreaths were laid by Mr H Whetter, on behalf of the Old Boys and Girls, and by AL Rowse, on behalf of the current pupils. 85 years later, the memorial with its 1939-45 update is still on the staircase of what is now Poltair School.

Then, in December 1921, both the Headmaster and Senior Mistress left to take appointments elsewhere, and, Mr WV Barritt and Miss A Bond were appointed to take their places. So began a new era for St Austell County School.

3. THE BARRITT/BOND YEARS.

Mr Barritt and Miss Bond held sway and dominated secondary education in St Austell for more than twenty years until Mr Barritt retired in 1944, with Miss Bond continuing until 1950. The first ten or so years saw the further development of the Mixed School while, between them, they enabled the division into the Boys'/Girls' Schools to be completed smoothly and harmoniously in 1933.

By 1922 pupil numbers had risen to 239, with roughly the same number of girls and boys. In 1924 the Ist Form entry was 59 with 24 being minor scholars, who had been successful in the County examination, and 32 fee paying pupils, who had passed the School entrance examination. There was one pupil under ten, and two transfers from other LEAs. By 1929 the School was considered to be over-full with 309 pupils, while in 1932/3, there was a record entry of 90 pupils, making a total of 345. Each year the number of fee payers exceeded the number of minor scholars, but not by much. Various strategies were employed to limit numbers – in 1928 there were no further entries during the school year and pupils from St Blazey, Tywardreath and Lostwithiel were not welcome until the separate schools were formed. In 1928 there was a request from Mr Barritt to the County for an extra member of staff because of VIth Form numbers and, while these numbers were not recorded, three pupils over the age of eighteen were allowed to remain at school to complete their studies in March 1933.

The curriculum did not develop much further as the basic subjects were already covered. New County regulations meant that from May 1922, schools had to be self sufficient as far as staffing was concerned. The exception was that a visiting Art teacher could be employed. This meant that the war-time innovations of shorthand, typing and book keeping were abandoned. Some experimentation was possible as long as it was covered by existing staff. Thus Chemistry and Physics, Nature Study and Botany, Economics and Roman History and Greek were introduced and taught for

The hedges have grown; the 'Old Kitchen', HM's room and cloakrooms have been added 1920s

The VIth Form 1926/7: RG Gale, P Hunkin, GL Cock, AJ Pascoe (Head Boy), RL Garratt, RJ Davies, JH Collins; Vandah Tyzzer (later to return as a teacher),Gladys Whale, Kathleen Whale, Mr Barritt, Mr Lodge (Form Master), Mollie Stamp (Head Girl), Marjorie Piper, Hilda Warrick

varying lengths of time in the 1920s. Music was in a different category and from 1926 pupils could pay 1 guinea per term for violin lessons. Apart from the choir which Miss Parry developed more specifically and to telling effect, whole school community singing was taken by the Headmaster on a Friday afternoon, as described by G.Golly, of IVA, in the 1928 Magazine:

Sing Song

Our School assemble in full force,
A great and gay community;
To sing perhaps, til we are hoarse,
The good old songs of unity.

For he who knows has laid it down
That singing is a tonic,
Chasing away each gloomy frown
And troubles that are chronic.

We children vote it ripping fun,
Our song books are before us;
Two hundred voices rise as one,
In a harmonious chorus.

As to staff conditions of service, it was decreed, in May 1924, that 65 was to be the upper age limit, except in very exceptional circumstances, and, in October 1925, the Burnham Scale of teachers' pay was adopted – in a few cases resulting in a decrease in salary. But at least it was now a national scale. Also in that year, following a master injuring his thumb while carrying out his duties, it was ruled that teachers were not covered by insurance under the Workmen's Compensation Act, and had to pay their own medical expenses, quite apart from being able claim any compensation.

There was inevitable change in staff and two stalwarts, who between them were to give over 80 years of service to the Schools, were appointed. Mr T Richardson came in 1923 to teach Physics and Geography, and Mr L Martin in 1924, to teach History. There was competition for staff vacancies. When Miss Scales (later to return as Mrs Goode) left in 1929, there were 110 applicants, and in June 1933, when a vacancy for a master in the new Boys' School was advertised, an incredible 616 applied.

In 1924, too, there was a change in the arrangements for caretaking, following a somewhat unsatisfactory spell. It was decided to appoint a husband

Teaching Staff 1924-5: Mr Saunders, Mr Parsons, Mr Martin, Mr Lodge, Mr Richardson, Mr Baker, Miss Rich, Miss Parry, Miss Bond, Mr Barritt, Miss Lewis, Miss Scales (later Mrs Goode)

and wife team to cover caretaking and cooking duties, and the first couple was appointed, from 70 applicants, in January 1925. Unfortunately, the caretaker did not turn out to be any more satisfactory than his predecessor, and as his wife had to go too, in 1928 Mr and Mrs Beable were appointed. They shared a combined salary of £224pa, plus free dinners, although the caretaker had to provide materials and pay two cleaners. This salary was calculated on the basis that a clay worker earned 42/- per week (£109pa) and the caretaker must be 'competent and intelligent to care for County property'.

By 1920, a report on old students which was not comprehensive, shows that St Austell was making its contribution both locally and nationally. 28 Old Girls held teaching posts in Cornwall and Devon, three were working in the Post Office, one in the Surveyor of Taxes Office and one in the District Education Office. Old Boys were employed as electricians, in the Bank of England, as teachers, a pianist, a decorative designer and a clerk in a Scottish mining company. There was also a total of fourteen old students still at college and university

in England. Major academic success came, first, in the person of AL Rowse who, by 1922, had gained an Open Scholarship at Christ Church, Oxford. He was subsequently to be awarded the first County Scholarship, of £60pa, to be won by the School, together with other scholarships to reach the £200pa minimum required to take up a place at Oxford. For several years a special committee of Governors met to raise further funds for him. The interest and concern they showed was rewarded in 1926, when he was awarded a Fellowship at All Souls. While not all attaining quite these national academic heights, other students also won acclaim. In 1923 Noreen Sweet was awarded a County University Scholarship and in 1929 HO Hooper won an Open Scholarship to Merton College, Oxford, together with three other scholarships amounting to £240pa. Initially the Governors had requested from the LEA a grant of £1.10/- for him to travel to Bodmin and lodge there, in order to take his scholarship examinations. In the same year Kathleen Miles won a state scholarship to Bristol and T Pascoe a free scholarship to Exeter (by now University College of the South West).

In 1925 a pupil, whose name is not recorded, came 26th of 400 applying for RAF entry, and, in 1933, T Williams came 32nd of 682 as an RAF apprentice, while Elsie Nancollas won a Domestic Science scholarship. These, and others, ensured that St Austell was not an academic back water.

The numbers taking and passing the Oxford and Cambridge Local and Higher Examinations (equivalent to GCSE and A Level) increased steadily. In 1921, 21 sat the Oxford Locals with sixteen being successful, while in 1931, 33 of the 38 candidates were successful in what was by then called School Certificate, with five being successful at Higher. It is difficult to make exact comparisons as records were not kept on a regular, standardised basis.

Throughout the 1920s there were references to the difficulties experienced by families in keeping their children in secondary education, with the fees rising from £3.10/-, in 1922, to £3.15/- in 1928. One problem was that some children, whose fathers had been killed in the War, were sponsored by various funds such as the United Services Fund and the Army Service Corps Fund. When these funds came to an end in the late 1920s, widowed mothers could no longer keep their children at school and there were requests, through the governing body, to the County for free places, which were usually granted for a limited period. There were also examples of poverty resulting from low wages or unemployment and, in 1928, Mr Barritt said he would pay the fees of a very promising boy, whose father could not pay, if the County would not. In January 1928, the County introduced a scheme of 50% fee remission for the third and subsequent child in the family, as long as there were three fee payers in the school at the same time. In June of the same year, another County decree stated that the maximum a school could levy on its pupils was 7/6d per year for games, together with a contribution towards a wreath for a fellow pupil, a bouquet for a special presentation and piano purchase or pavilion building, the latter being particularly pertinent for St Austell. Increasingly maintenance allowances were made by the County to needy families, requests for which were presented to the County by the Governors. In 1922 there was the occasional request but by 1929, 48 pupils (38 minor scholars and ten fee payers) were granted mostly between £1.10/- and £4 per

NEW BOY (looking at boys' new tennis court after a heavy shower.)
" 'Spose those white lines in the swimming bath there are for water polo ! "

From the School Magazine Spring 1924

year, with the occasional £7.10/- or £15. In 1931 a minor scholar was granted free spectacles and from 1921 minor scholars had free transport if they lived more than three miles from School.

Even so, much Governors' business time was still taken up with constant reference to non-payment of fees, often because the family had moved away, but more frequently because the pupils had left having gained positions in the Post Office, banks or the GWR. There was also a number of children who were away from school for one or two terms because of sickness.

There was positive encouragement for children to save and in May 1933, the School National Savings Association was formed with twenty fortunate children having cards to record their saved sixpences.

Extra curricular activities continued to thrive. Provision for games proceeded apace. In the Spring

The victorious Hockey XI County Champions 1923: F Matthews, J Edwards, M Paul, Miss Parry, M Varcoe, M Gale; M Best, L Williams, M Clyma (Capt), E Paul; E Garner, G Church

of 1922 the girls' tennis court at the front of the School was finished and the boys' tennis court and cricket practice ground were under construction. By 1923 the netball court had been extended and tar sprayed and plans were in hand for a sport's pavilion. Initially the girls were the leading lights being County Hockey Champions for three years in succession and winning the Hockey Cup outright in 1924. This, in spite of the fact that, according to the account of a contemporary, the game was played 'by beautiful creatures from middle-class St Austell homes'! In 1927 the football XI won the County Shield, while the hockey and netball teams lost in their finals. Success continued for all three teams until the division of the School in 1933. Swimming sports were introduced in 1923 and, with a few interruptions, were a regular feature of the sporting calendar. Indeed, it was taken so seriously that in 1924 a 'half holiday was promised to the form which had every boy and girl a swimmer'. At first, in 1923, a very successful Sports was held at Porthpean and a contemporary account, again from a School Magazine, outlines some of the difficulties. After hiring buses to get the children

to Porthpean, 'the work of conveying the competitors to the starting boat was soon begun and carried through by young oarsmen, whose eagerness compensated somewhat for their lack of dexterity. In some cases, a knowledge of oars seemed to be merely academic.' The whole activity was aided by Mr Howard Dunn from his ketch, 'Theodora', which was anchored in the bay. By 1928 the event had moved to Charlestown where it was not necessary to use starting boats. Athletics, too, were held on the town cricket field just down the road, until 1926 when new facilities enabled the School's own field to be used. Mr Richardson introduced boxing in 1923, and rugby was played by 1925, not, apparently, with a great deal of success. In 1930 the annual cricket match against Bodmin School at Lanhydrock, courtesy of Viscount Clifden, was described by the Headmaster as being an event which was 'balm to my soul'. Folk dancing was gaining support and teams regularly took part in County Festivals with the highlight being in 1933 when the folk dancers were to represent the School on Flora Day, presumably at Helston, but not specified.

Above: *Football XI 1926/7 having won the County Shield with Mr Richardson and Mr Martin*
Below: *Swimming Sports Programme 1925*

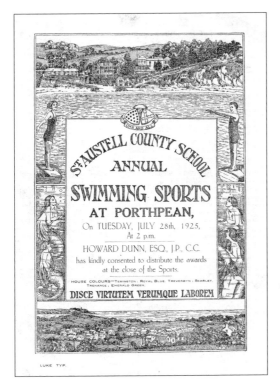

The prowess of the School Choir, and its impact on the county scene, continued throughout the 1920s and early '30s. The Vintner Shield for mixed choirs was won nearly every year, and in 1931, it was suggested that St Austell keep the award and provide the County with a new one – there were fifteen spaces for winners' names, and St Austell had won thirteen times. Much of the credit for this must go to the skill and enthusiasm of Miss Parry, but, undoubtedly, Mr Barritt's interest, together with his Friday afternoon sing-a-longs played their part.

Annual School dramatic presentations became the norm with productions ranging from AA Milne to Shakespeare, by way of Greek plays and GB Shaw. The opening of the new Hall, in 1927, was marked by a production of *Quality Street* by JM Barrie, which was also presented in Truro as the School's contribution to Education Week.

From 1924 a list of the school rules was posted in every class room, including compulsory games, unless really physically unfit. Stars and stripes, the system both to reward and to chastise, was well established by 1928 and continued as an integral

Above: *Swimming Sports at Porthpean using a starting boat 1920s (Mr Dunn's 'Theodora' ?)*
Below: *Sports Day 1926* **Right:** *Sports Day 1926 Fiercely contested Egg and Spoon Race*

Above: *Tea interval during a 1920s Sports Day.
The bench was later part of an Obstacle Race*
Below: *Tewington Tug o' War Team 1928. Fred
Bennetto was part of the team, front row, third from left*

part of the calculation of House points until well into the 1960s. School uniform was important and strict rules aimed to ensure that the pupils were neat and tidy. By 1930, the girls had changed from navy blue to bottle green tunics and blazers, with black felt hats in winter and panama hats in the summer. The boys wore short trousers until they were about fourteen with purple blazers and caps and purple and yellow striped ties. From 1924, in line with other schools in Cornwall, an Armistice Day Service was held annually. The General Strike of 1926 did not affect attendance, according to an entry in the Log Book.

Increasingly pupils were taken on trips both within and outside the County in order to open their eyes to the wider world and to improve their career prospects. In May 1924, 122 pupils and six teachers went to the Wembley Exhibition, with 46 following the next year. 1926 saw a party visiting the Theatre Royal in Plymouth for a production of *Julius Caesar*. A party of boys went to the GWR Workshops in Swindon in 1929 and, two years later, another group visited the Telephone Exchange – 'Here we were astonished to see Paynter and Menear gaily sending telegrams

Above: *Cricket XI late 1920s with Mr Richardson*
Below: *Girls' Cricket Team 1920 with Miss Parry (courtesy Sue Sharland)*

Folk Dance Festival at St Austell 1926(?)
Opposite page: *Lady Mary Trefusis provides the musical support*

Choir with Vintner Shield 1924 with Miss Parry

Above: *Cast of Troy Town by Quiller Couch 1920*
Below: *Cast of The Rivals by Sheridan 1923*

Above: *Cast of Quality Street by JM Barrie 1927*

to such places as Newcastle.' A mixed party of 150 pupils was entertained by Fry's Cocoa at Somervale in Bristol in May 1933, which must have been a considerable undertaking. In between there were trips to the cinema, local dramatic productions and form visits to places of local interest such as Lanhydrock in 1933.

The curriculum continued to be enriched by visiting speakers covering a wealth of subjects ranging from *India* in 1925 to Rev. BS Watkins' racey account of *Life in Nigeria* in 1932, from *Morocco* in January 1928, organised by Mrs Treffry, to *The Shakespearean Play* by Mr Roger Williams in 1926. JWF Cardwell, in 1930, gave a well presented and much appreciated talk on the Overseas Settlement Department and in January 1933, Mr Fred Maddison of the International Arbitration League talked about *Mandates*. In 1931 AL Rowse returned to present *English Poetry in relation to English History* and in 1932 a cine film on *Unknown Nepal* was followed by a lecture. The increase of 'visual aids' as an element of outside lectures brought its own problems and by 1929 the Headmaster was stressing the neces-

sity for curtains or screens on the windows of the new Hall.

The provision of school dinners continued to be a constant cause for concern, and a drain on resources. However, with the improved conditions in the 'Old Kitchen', numbers continued to grow until, by 1928, there were two sessions, with 55 pupils taking the first and 97 the second. Such was the pressure that when plans were being drawn up for the adaptation/building of separate schools in 1929, an urgent request was made to the County that a new Dining Hall should be built first. In November 1932, this new building began to provide meals for 160 boys/girls, with everything on the same floor and prefects no longer having to work the lift. It was described, in the School Magazine, as being 'spacious, light and airy with cream walls and orange tablecloths. Tumblers were green and there were flowers according to the season'. Dinners cost 3/- per week, and provision was also made for pupils to bring sandwiches. Cynthia Sleeman (1928-33) remembers Mr Barritt frequently stressing at Prayers that jam sandwiches should not be brought for dinner, but so often, she

Building of the Sports Pavilion by the boys of IIIB and IVB 1924/5

Below: *Completed Sports Pavilion 1925*

Above: *Opening of Sports Pavilion 1925*
Below: *Drill in the Wet Weather Shelter, early 1930s*

St. Austell County School

The buildings with the new Hall 1927

says, families could not afford anything else.

Very slowly, but surely, improvements in technical help towards the efficient running of the School were seen – although frequent forward looking requests to the County did not receive an immediate, positive response. The Library grant rose from £7.10/- in 1921 to £15pa in 1925, but requests for shelving or bookcases were not successful. In January 1926 a request for a Roneo Copier (£31.10/-, less 10%) was not approved, but in 1929 a wireless set, at a cost of £30, was up and running, albeit with generally poor reception. This was bought from a percentage of the fees charged for Music lessons, and was for use in the Junior School for History, Geography and Music. However, in 1931, the whole School was able to hear an inspiring Empire Day message by Lord Jellicoe, with much improved reception. Frequent requests for a new sewing machine because the existing one had 'worn out', fell on deaf ears. The chore of cutting the grass on the playing fields was resolved, to some extent, in May 1932, by the purchase of an Atco de Luxe 36 motor mower for £106, by the Headmaster, hoping for Governors'

approval! In 1926 Mr Barritt also bought a grand piano for the bargain price of £35, which, no doubt aided his Friday afternoon sing-a-long.

The thorny question of the supply of water was an ongoing one in the 1920s, with the Headmaster recommending a change from the UDC to the RDC suppliers at an extra cost of £10pa. The provision of electric light for the whole School was not resolved either, although, in January 1927, the Governors insisted that it must be installed in the new Hall. There was no telephone nor clerical support, for the Headmaster at this time. A request to the County, in 1926, brought the response that he must use a pupil!

In 1931 the lower playing field was levelled by utilising a large quantity of earth from Port Gribbon House on the corner of Hillside Road, but there were complaints about the mess which resulted. At the same time a useless piece of land near the Brewery was levelled and concreted to increase playground area. In May 1933, sixteen unemployed men levelled the hockey field at a cost of two good meals a day (12/-) and the hire of a horse and cart (£3). This left the School with

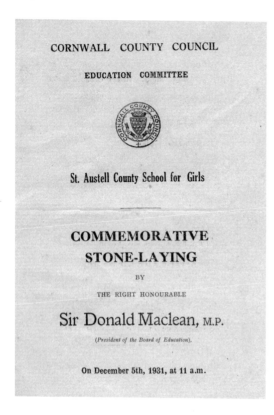

CORNWALL COUNTY COUNCIL

EDUCATION COMMITTEE

St. Austell County School for Girls

COMMEMORATIVE STONE-LAYING

BY

THE RIGHT HONOURABLE

Sir Donald Maclean, M.P.

(President of the Board of Education).

On December 5th, 1931, at 11 a.m.

Laying the Foundation Stone for the new Girls' School 1931

a £90 debt, but it was considered to be a necessary expense.

Improvements to the existing premises in the 1920s were based, very much, on the self help principle. The building of the pavilion at the top of the playing field, is probably the best example. In January 1924, the cost was estimated to be £120 and the County was asked to provide help. The boys of IIIB and IVB, including the researcher's father, Fred Bennetto, overseen by Mr Hopkins, the Woodwork master, had completed the job for £195. It was opened on July 2nd 1925, by Mr CV Thomas, Chairman of the Higher Education Committee. Each boy was given a photograph as a souvenir. Wet weather shelters, too, were needed for dinner hours – presumably the pupils were not allowed into their form rooms when not actually being taught – and in January 1926, masters and boys were to complete the work with the County providing the materials, which included asbestos roofing materials. These took rather longer to be

completed than expected as agreement with the County was not reached until early in 1930, and on December 28th severe gales caused so much damage that the work had to be started again. The flag pole, together with a flag, both donated by individual Governors, eventually was in place in June 1928.

Alongside this development greater schemes were being discussed at County level. By April 1924 it was recognised, at local as well as County level, that major changes were required, and required as a matter of some urgency. The School, which had been built in 1908 for 200 pupils, was bursting at the seams with well in excess of that number and with no likelihood of demand decreasing. A meeting of the County Buildings Committee with the Chairman and Vice-Chairman of St Austell Governors agreed that there were only two options – a separate school for the girls, costing some £8,000 or a major extension of the current building to include a Hall and Dining Hall, costing some £7,500. The general conclusion was that separate schools was the desirable option, with much emphasis, again, on the unsuitability of mixed education, in spite of the apparent success of the School. The LEA, in October 1924, could not countenance a new school in St Austell when the needs of Truro and Saltash were much more pressing. In January 1925, however, plans for a new Hall, to be used for assembly as well as a gymnasium, were accepted and by early 1927, during a period of depression and economy, it was opened. There was some local hostility at such money being spent on a relatively small proportion of the local population, and, consequently, some of the more lavish plans, such as a School bell, an oak honours board and a grand piano or organ, were quietly shelved. The Hall was built where it could be used by separate schools should this be the development, and as it later was. When, in 1929, there were just over 300 pupils, the LEA recognised the need, and plans for a new Girls' School and the adaptation of the existing premises for Boys were underway.

The Foundation Stone was laid in 1931 with the School Magazine not recording unmitigated satisfaction: 'Before long we shall be preparing for unwelcome separation.' Building work took about two years with all the obvious disruption. Improvements in one area only resulted in the inadequacies of other parts being highlighted. For instance, the UDC relaid the approaches to the School in January 1933 which made the playground surfaces look even worse, causing Mr Barritt to bewail the fact that he was not able to use another group of unemployed men for the repair work. However, the Direct Labour Team was used to distemper part of the Boys' School which had been altered internally. Difficulties were encountered in securing a notable person to open the Girls' School in September 1933, and eventually it was decided to ask the local MP, Maurice Petherick. An unforeseen bonus occurred when the Prince of Wales visited the Royal Cornwall Show, held in St Austell that year, and wished to view the work done by the group of unemployed men who had levelled the hockey field. He was shown the new Hall and the Dining Hall and signed the new Girls' School Visitor's Book.

A major effort during the summer holidays enabled the Girls' School to be ready for the beginning of term on September 12th 1933 and this was followed by a busy settling-in process and preparation for the official Opening. Miss Bond reports that, 'It was a very pleasant occasion and everything ran smoothly..........We entertained about 260 adults to tea and were a crowded but jolly party – and 150 girls had refreshments on the lawn in front of the Hall.'

Visit of the Prince of Wales 1933
He came to the Royal Cornwall Show at St Austell and
wanted to see the work of the group of unemployed men.
His signature is the first in the Girls' School
Visitor's Book

4. SEPARATE SCHOOLS

– BUT STILL, IN MANY WAYS, TOGETHER.

The fact that the heads of the newly separated Schools had already worked for more than ten years as Head Master and Senior Mistress was a major factor in the separation of the Schools not being as definitive as it might have been.

During the first year, 1933/4, there were joint assemblies but after that the increased numbers, 375, made this impractical. A joint Speech Day was last held in December 1934 when, again, the logistics of larger numbers forced separation. School Magazines were a joint production until, in 1936, the Girls' School produced its first. Combined Athletics and Swimming Sports events continued throughout the 1930s. The Dining Hall enjoyed mixed use until 1955, with, initially, boys and girls sitting on opposite sides of the tables, and, later, on separate tables. Both Schools shared use of the Hall for radio broadcasts of national occasions such as the Proclamation of Edward

VIII and the launching of the Queen Mary, but it was also used separately for assemblies, drama performances, Speech Days and other events special to each School.

Staffing issues and difficulties did not disappear with the formation of separate Schools. Some members of staff were shared, for instance Mr Martin taught some History in the Girls' School. Pupils were still admitted from the age of eight and the problems of teaching classes with an age range of eight to eleven were great. In 1936 these difficulties were overcome to some extent by the Girls' amalgamating with the Boys' School to establish a 'prep' department for under elevens. Presumably this did not provoke the usual criticism of mixed classes as that was the norm in the Elementary Schools. There was some debate in the Girls' School concerning the provision of Latin. In some quarters it was thought that it helped to

The new Girls' School 1933

Above: *The opening of the new Girls' School building, September 1933. FR Pascoe (Secretary of Education) on the extreme left next to Miss Bond. Sir Arthur Quiller Couch on the extreme right.*
Below: *The new Dining Hall for combined use from 1932*

An informal group of staff of the Girls' School in what came to be known as the Quad 1930s. Included are: Miss Bracher, Miss Goldsworthy, Miss Draycon, Miss Parry, Miss Watkins (later Mrs Truscott) and Miss Saint.

create too academic an environment and that the substitution of shorthand and typing would be much preferable. Miss Bond had her own views on this. While not agreeing with the premise that it is good for pupils to have to learn what they dislike, she had no intention of allowing shorthand and typing to become part of the main School curriculum. 'These subjects are of little educational or intellectual value and if they find a place in our curriculum next year, it will be in the post Certificate form, ie the Sixth' she said at the 1936 Speech Day. She also feared that she would find it increasingly difficult to cater for a VIth Form without extra staff, although she frequently deplored the fact that so many girls left after the Vth Form, and some even before. The Boys' School, too, experienced difficulties with teaching a small VIth Form and much of this teaching, apparently, was done during the masters' free periods. It is remarkable the level of achievement attained in this way. In 1938 an extra member of staff was authorised for each School by the County. Mr RW Hart was appointed to teach Science and Maths in the Boys' School, and Miss McVicar (later Mrs Babbage and

later still Mrs Clymo) was appointed, from over 100 applicants, to teach Latin in the Girls' School. Anecdotal evidence from Old Boys, points to the huge success of Mr W Phelps who made French appear so easy that all boys took it at School Certificate and only a very few were not successful. Both Schools continued to follow a broad based academic curriculum, with Woodwork for Junior Boys and Domestic Science for Junior Girls, the latter still at West Hill. While masters, obviously, could marry, mistresses could not, and, until the Second World War, they were required to resign on marriage.

The curriculum continued to be broadened by the encouraging of outside lecturers, some bringing films and other visual aids. Perhaps the most notable was in June 1938 when SPB Mais, the noted writer and broadcaster, talked to both Schools on *Getting our money's worth*. His 'bright and breezy style' made it a 'great treat'.

Aids to give more variety to teaching and to make the administration of the Schools more effective, were slow in coming. However, in 1936 both Schools acquired new HMV wireless sets, partly from their School Funds, and they were used for main stream subjects as well as Music and World Affairs. In 1934 the Girls' School requested an Ellams Duplicating Machine, for 4 guineas, from the Governors. This would eliminate the inconvenience of having to go to the Boys' School to use theirs, and, early in 1939, they also requested 50% of the cost of an epidiascope. We can assume that these requests were granted as they were not repeated, but it is not certain. Regular grants were made to each School for their libraries, for instance the Boys' received £15 in 1935, but neither was successful in obtaining a room for a Library. Indeed, the Girls' acquired a set of Encyclopaedia in 1937, but requests for more shelving fell on deaf ears. In January 1938 both Mr Barritt and Miss Bond requested telephones for their Schools, but, again, both were rejected by the County. Secretarial assistance for both Heads was still casual and unpaid.

Results in public examinations continued to improve. In School Certificate 28 boys, being the whole of the Vth Form, sat in 1934, with 27 being successful, while fourteen girls were entered and twelve passed. Five years later, in 1939, 37 boys were entered and 30 were successful, while all of the 21 girls who entered passed. The numbers entered for Higher, the A Level equivalent, were more patchy, but by 1939, three boys and three girls were entered and all were successful.

There was a steady stream of pupils from both Schools who won County University Scholarships as well as special Scholarships or Exhibitions to various Higher Education establishments. Both boys and girls proceeded to universities and colleges and, in 1938, Margaret Galley was the first girl to achieve Oxbridge entrance to Lady Margaret Hall, Oxford. There is mention of sources of extra funding available for these students. In 1938 the St Austell Lectures Committee gave £30.17/4d for deserving members of the Schools attending university and in 1936 there is a record of the School Loan Fund having loaned £77.10/-, with no apparent security or time limit. Many entered the Civil Service, mostly the Clerical Class, by passing national, competitive examinations. Teaching was the regular professional destination, especially for girls, and many began as probationers in local Elementary Schools. In the 1930s there were many more local, family run businesses and these provided apprenticeships and employment for many. Some were offered professional training such as auctioneers, estate agents and surveyors while many others became clerks, receptionists and shop assistants. The GWR, Boots the Chemists, the GPO and, of course, ECLP and other smaller clay companies were some of the larger, national organisations which continued to recruit locally. There was a further trickle of boys entering the Services, especially the RAF, and in 1939 73 boys were listed as being in all branches of the Services. While information is by no means complete, clearly both Schools continued to contribute able employees both locally and nationally.

Pupils continued to travel beyond Cornwall as well as within the County, to expand their experience and take part in national events. In 1934 boys of Form IA visited the magistrates' court and senior boys attended a special demonstration of 'Safety Services' at Hill & Phillips, followed by tea in the newly opened Richards & Dyer Café. Each year about 30 girls took part in the Cornwall Folk Dance Festival at different venues in the County. There were County Expeditions to the GWR at Swindon, with 92 boys going in 1935. Regular trips to the cinema and to dramatic performances were enjoyed by both Schools, such as the first performance in the Cornwall Shakespearean Festival of *The Merchant of Venice*, held in the open air at Trevarrick Hall in July 1935, when all the pupils attended. Again it was parties from both Schools which visited the archaeological excavations at Castle Dore in 1936. Later in the same year, 30 boys and senior girls saw Dorothy Round and other leading tennis players in a Covered Court Tournament at the Cornish Riviera Club. George V's Silver Jubilee, in 1935, saw each pupil receive a beaker. The Coronation of George VI, in 1937, was followed by an Empire Youth Rally with two boys and two girls travelling to London for the festivities. A party of 88 boys with five masters also travelled to London to see the decorations – a venture which was deemed to be a great success, if a little tiring for the younger ones! According to our information, the Girls' School took part in the first French Exchange, in 1936, with a girl from Le Havre and, at Easter 1938, a party of VIth Form girls went to Paris with Miss Lewis and Miss Stockley – the first record we have of an

Hockey XI 1934 having beaten Truro 5-0 and won the County Championship: D Hicks, P Roberts, Miss Parry, D Roberts, M Prophet; L Pearce, E Bounsall, B Wilson (Capt), E McPherson, J Lintern; D Phillips, C Furse

overseas trip.

On the sports field St Austell continued to make its mark. The football XI made its customary appearances in the County Finals. The Girls' hockey XI won the County Championship four times, most conclusively in 1938, defeating Truro 8-1. Boys' hockey was introduced in 1936 with four boys eventually progressing to the 1st XI of St Lukes College in Exeter – William Sheaff, Jack Trevenna, Archie Smith and Denys Sandercock. Once the hard court had been completed, in 1935, netball flourished with the positive support of Miss Bond who said in 1936, 'Netball, in my opinion, is one of the finest games for growing girls, but I have my doubts about hockey.' Joint Athletic Sports Meetings were held each year and in 1935, the event was so popular that there were '230 for tea – we sold 60 tickets on the field – there was a shortage of cups.' By 1937 the levelling of the field which had begun in 1922, had been completed and 46 events were held. Miss McDowell, the County PT organiser, presented the prizes and spoke of 'this School, which more than any other, has shown such an incredible amount of energy to

make its own ground into a real sports ground for the boys and girls.' Swimming Sports continued to be held annually at Charlestown and, while there did not appear to be the same emphasis on children learning to swim, Miss Bond was able to boast that in 1937 80% of girls could swim. Boys' cricket did not make any headlines during this period, but one Old Boy, KA Thomas, remembers Mr Martin and Mr Adams playing against Harold Larwood and Bill Voce – where, when and why is not recorded.

The choirs enjoyed different sorts of success in the 1930s. They could no longer compete for the Vintner Shield, which they had dominated in the 1920s, as it was a competition for mixed schools and the 'togetherness' did not extend that far. However, separately they continued to win certificates at County Music Festivals. Both Schools continued to produce a dramatic performance as part of their respective Speech Day celebrations with the Girls performing *Pride and Prejudice* with the first all girl cast, in 1937. The Old Austellians gave regular performances with a mixed cast, throughout the 1930s. The Debating and Literary

DISCE VIRTUTEM VERUMQUE LABOREM

The ST. AUSTELL COUNTY SCHOOL ANNUAL ATHLETIC SPORTS

THURSDAY, JUNE 16th, 1938,
at 2 p.m.

On the SCHOOL PLAYING FIELD.

MONSIEUR J. PIERROT

has kindly consented to present the awards.

Royal Blue. Emerald Green. Scarlet.
TEWINGTON · TRENANCE · TREVERBYN

Sports Day Programme 1938 This was still a joint activity
NB the cover has not been amended to include the Girls' School building!

Prefects 1934 although the Schools were separate they were still photographed together for the joint Magazine:
Back Row: *J Oates, JT Williams, CH Trevail, CR Allen, LJ Sweet, AP Reynolds (Head Boy), EK May, HG Lidgey, TW Grose, AG Clook* **Front Row:** *Ruth Gordon, Muriel Vanson, Enid McPherson, Effie Bounsall, Betty Wilson (Head Girl), Jenefer Nancollas, Mabel Lobb, Carol Furse*

Societies appear to have been largely joint operations with the debates ranging from in 1934: 'That Great Britain should pursue a policy of isolationism rather than collective security' to, the following year: 'That we should go abroad for our summer holidays'.

The 1930s, clearly, were not easy times for families living in the St Austell district, as with everywhere else during what became known as the Depression. Maintenance and travel grants continued to be made on application to the Governors, and, in 1938, 26 were made to boys and 22 to girls. Parental occupations of the recipients were varied, from clay labourer to fisherman, herdsman to engine driver, mason to electrician. Annually special grants were made to individuals for glasses, and free milk clearly was available as, in 1935, the Clerk to the Governors was authorised to deal with applications. The major change came in 1933 when following Circular 1421 from the County, minor scholars, who had passed the County examination, were no longer guaranteed a free place. They became known as 'Special Places' and a charge was made towards school fees according to

parental income. There was complete exemption from fees for a family earning £3-£4 per week, with one child. There was an appropriate scale thereafter. At the same time the County hoped to set fees at a minimum rate of 15 guineas per year. 'Q', Vice-Chairman of the Education Committee, wrote to the Chairman expressing his disapproval of putting obstacles in the way of promising pupils saying, 'it is diminishing the brain of the nation at its source'. This means testing of minor scholars may have been a retrograde step, but it was a difficult time economically. In 1931 the pay of teachers, along with other centrally funded occupations, was cut by 15%.

School dinners flourished in the new Dining Hall, and, by early 1936 the numbers had increased so much that a new, larger gas oven was purchased for £31.9/- – the smaller one it replaced going to another school which needed it. Contemporaries record that it was the only time that boys and girls could meet, socially, during school time. At first they sat each side of the same table but Mick Lomer (1936-43) remembers their sitting at separate tables. Reports of the food vary. 'Adequate,

The Dining Hall in November 1939 with the boys and girls sharing as they were to until 1955. (Courtesy Cornish Guardian)

always nourishing, seldom exciting' from Thomas Clemens (1930-37) to Marian Yelland's opinion that the meals were not very good –'I couldn't eat corned beef for years afterwards', while Mrs Beable's 'lovely bread and butter pudding' is remembered with affection by many girls. At this stage girls were put on rotas to help with the washing up and there are definite memories of evasion tactics, including hiding in cupboards – we have reliable but anonymous records!

There were inspections of both Schools in late 1935 and early 1936 and, while the reports overall were good, some deficiencies in the Girls' School building were underlined, which is rather surprising considering how new the building was. Particularly, it was pointed out, there were no facilities for teaching Housecraft, there was no Rest Room and there was no hot water in the cloakrooms. A new Housecraft Centre, which had been requested in 1934 to save the trek to West Hill, was approved by the County in 1937. However, early in 1938, Miss Bond admitted that she had misread the plans and that the entrance was on the 'wrong side' of the building, in other

words, the Boys' side. It was too late then for changes and the building which was in use in September 1938, forever after faced the 'wrong way'. The new Domestic Science Room, as it was called, did not please everyone. Miss Bond reported to the Cornish Guardian in December 1937, 'The younger members of the School will miss the leisurely stroll to and from the Cookery Centre (at West Hill) and that unauthorised prowl around the fascinating stalls of Messrs Woolworths.' The Rest Room did not materialise before 1939, but the Gas Co did install two Ascot Water Heaters in the Girls' cloakroom.

The building of the Girls' School had brought with it attendant difficulties. The rubbish left from the building works was a constant source of irritation, as was the state of the road in front of the Girls' School. The UDC had been given a slice of land to widen and improve Tregonissey Road but it took a long time for the work to be completed, and the approaches were a mess for several years. The state of the playgrounds left much to be desired – the Boys' had not been renewed since the building work of 1925. However, in 1934 a

43

paved play area for the girls, presumably the area later known as the Quad, was completed for £82, but the request for a covered way to the Hall never materialised. Work was done, in 1934, to repair the boys' bicycle shed damaged in the gales of the late 1920s, and there were plans to build a new one for the girls, which was not completed until 1938. Progress was made in the provision of hard sports surfaces for both Schools – the Girls' netball court being ready in 1935 and the Boys' tennis court in 1936.

Other buildings could cause annoyance. The new Football Stand on the Town Football Ground opposite the Schools caused Mr Barritt to comment in 1934 that he did not know how the UDC 'came to perpetrate such a blot on the landscape'!

One event which caused much excitement and comment was the fire in the Boys' School. A lengthy and humorous account, in the Boys' Magazine of 1938, tells of the events of February 8th when something went wrong with the heating apparatus causing the caretaker to fear that the boiler would blow up. Mr Barritt, who was at a Rotary Lunch, was summoned to deal with the crisis. He and Mr Lodge, not realising that the caretaker had raked out the red hot cinders from the boiler, went to the stoke hole and, when they opened the door, there was a mini explosion which caused the cinders to fall onto 'a pile of fuel consisting of coal, coke, straw, brown paper, boxes and packing. This obligingly caught fire and gave off dense clouds of smoke.' The boys were sent home while the caretaker and some of the prefects attempted, unsuccessfully, to put out the fire. The Fire Brigade was then called, alerting boys in Fore Street to return to School to watch, but the hydrants produced only a 'thin trickle of water'. Firemen then 'donning smoke helmets and braving the elements' brought much of the burning debris from the stoke hole and threw it out of the window on the other side of the corridor. By this time a number of boys had gathered as spectators and they were used to form 'a chain of boys, and buckets of water were passed along the line to the seat of the fire, to make sure it was definitely out'. Unfortunately, the Fire Brigade had obtained 'a good stream of water' from elsewhere, 'but it was so unexpected that it began to flood the premises. By the time the water had been turned off, the hoses collected and the Brigade left, the

crowd had also dispersed, and the only people to be seen about the building, were the caretaker and the various self appointed minor officials assisting him to clear up the mess.' And, finally, 'what about the three new fire extinguishers in the Hall? In the excitement, these had actually been overlooked'.

The event provoked 'Teraphim and Seraphim' to pen the following in the Girls' Magazine of May 1938:

A is the Anxiety everyone felt,
B is the Boiler which started to melt.
C is the Cheers when the fire brigade came,
D is the Day which brought the school fame.
E is the Excitement which then did prevail
F is for Fearless – each carrying pail.
G is the Gas-mask each fireman wore.
H is the Hose, well to the fore.
I is the Imp who three cheers did raise,
J is the Joy as the boys viewed the blaze.
K is for Kitchen – the only safe place,
L for Lab. windows with many a face.
M is for the Masters who flitted about,
N is for Nuisances who wouldn't clear out.
O is for Oxygen of which there was need.
P is for Prefects – hard workers indeed!
Q is for Query of how it all started,
R is a Rest cure for the faint hearted.
S is the Smoke rising higher and higher,
T is the Triumph of quenching the fire.
U is the Upset – (what next will there be?)
V is for Visitors who hastened to see.
W's for Windows through which they all crawl,
X for the Xtra help for which many call.
Y is for Yells when the blaze was all done,
Z ends the tale how the boys had great fun.

The 2nd St Austell County School Scout Troop was formed and registered in December 1936 under Mr PL Martin and quickly settled to make an important contribution both to the School and the town. By 1939 there were two King's Scouts, J Kernick and AR Wilton, but a request, in May 1939, for support to send a scout to New Zealand for the Jamboree, had to be rejected as there were no funds available. They did suffer, however, from a lack of permanent premises, presumably because the Scout Leader, at that time, was not a member of the School staff and therefore a room in the School was not appropriate.

Thomas Clemens remembers the School being assembled on the playing field to watch the airship R101 fly over St Austell Bay in about 1934 and there are memories of other less worthy deeds. John Rockey (1938-41) tells of a master who drove a Baby Austin 7 to school and parked it in the playground. 'I recall watching with glee, as some twenty seniors got round it at break time, and carried it bodily round the corner and hid it'! This feat, according to a reliable, but again anonymous witness, was repeated in the 1960s. John Rockey also refers to the 'strictly illegal school smoking club' which had its headquarters in the Groundsman's hut behind the pavilion, with the Groundsman as President.

By the end of the summer term 1939 the LEA was already getting itself prepared for war, in spite of Chamberlain's 'Peace in our Time', following the Munich Agreement of September 1938. Plans had been drawn up for Air Raid Precautions in October and in May 1939, proposals were being made to respond to a national emergency, especially with the formation of the Evacuation Sub Committee. However, in spite of the number of boys already as members of the armed forces, it is doubtful if many of the Schools' population expected the outbreak of war so soon.

5. THE IMPACT OF WAR.

In many ways the basic work of both schools continued throughout the War years with young people continuing to be taught an academic curriculum and achieving much success. But in other ways the effects were profound. This war, from 1939-45, was quite different from the First World War in that it had a much more immediate effect on the population at home, and these effects, to varying degrees, were felt in St Austell.

From late 1939 children were evacuated to St Austell from the major cities. At first more than 100 boys and girls came from inner city areas of London as part of an official exercise and other individual families chose to move en bloc to a safer environment. While the first wave tended to drift back during what was known as the 'phoney war', more came to take their place, particularly a large contingent from Bristol in May 1941, from Merrywood, St George and Fairfield Schools. This meant that numbers in both Schools were well over 200 throughout the War years, with the peak, in September 1941, of 330 in the Boys' School and 271 in the Girls'. In May 1942, there were 63 evacuees in the Boys' School and 71 in the Girls'. The situation was exacerbated in 1941, by the arrival of 200 boys together with thirteen members of staff from Sutton High School, Plymouth, who were based at the Boys' School. The resulting pressure on accommodation was, obviously, huge. Classes were held in every available square foot with, for instance, two classes permanently in the pavilion. The space under the balcony in the Hall was blocked off and became a classroom with two more classes in the Hall itself, but still there was not enough room. Tregonissey Institute became the home of the Boys' Ist Forms, which caused some parental anxiety because of their isolation, but they returned to the main building once a week for an Assembly, a singsong and some PE. Sutton had to travel further to the Methodist Sunday Schools at Carclaze and Bridge in Mount Charles. However all were accommodated and a shift system was avoided. 'It was', wrote Mr CF Jones, the Headmaster of Sutton, in *A School at War,* 'a triumph of improvisation on the part of the County School. Mr Barritt crowned his efforts on our behalf by handing over to me his own office.' As time went on Sutton gradually were able to concentrate their teaching rooms in the town at, for instance, Mengu Hall and No1 Trevarthian Road, abandoning the further flung areas, keeping their headquarters in the County School and sharing the use of both the Boys' and Girls' laboratories. Sutton was not the only school evacuated in the district. King's School, Canterbury was at the Carlyon Bay Hotel and there was, apparently, a little friction over the shared use of, for instance, the town cricket field.

While the Girls' School suffered less than the Boys', Mr Jones recalls that 'their willingness was as great, and the unfailing kindness and good humour of Miss Bond acted as a tonic. When the billeting situation or the latest edition of the time-table reduced me to a hair-tearing wreck, I would put my work aside and repair to her charming room with a demand for tea, and would return again to my work with renewed vigour.'

There was pressure, too, on arrangements for school meals. In February 1941 there were 260 for lunch and, although the kitchen was equipped only for 200, they felt that they were managing quite well. The opening of the British Restaurant in Zion Methodist Church Sunday School in September 1941 was a boon but there were still 285 to be catered for and these numbers were sustained throughout the War. Considering food rationing and the shortage of food, Mrs Beable's meals were a triumph of adaptability and mostly favourably received. There was a major organisational change on January 1st 1945 when the LEA took over school meals. Miss Bond asked the County for some compensation for monies spent on refurbishment of equipment, but nothing was forthcoming.

There was also not enough equipment. Sutton brought their own school furniture but no transport had been available in the heavily bombed Plymouth of 1941 and the china clay industry came to the rescue sending lorries to collect the school furniture such as desks. 'Everything we touched for the next fortnight left a white mark, but it soon wore off.' Mr Barritt and Miss Bond, mean-

The arrival of evacuees meant reams of instructions and documentation from various government departments.

while, had to acquire from somewhere, anywhere, enough desks and chairs for their evacuee population. While there were arrangements nationally between LEAs to cover costs and, in some cases, children's clothing, there did not appear to be practical help in gaining basic equipment. Cornwall's problem was massive – by the end of May 1941, the county had a secondary school population of 3,988 with an added 3,116 evacuees!

The experiences of the evacuees in their billeting varied enormously. Nancy Perry (Ashdown) from Merrywood School in Bristol lived with five different families during her three years from 1941-4 while Michael Wilkinson with his friend Bob Morgan, also from Bristol, were 'the luckiest of them all' being billeted with Gwendoline Howells' chauffeur and his wife in what is now the Porth Avallen Hotel – 'we could not have chosen a more beautiful spot to live in.' From the information we have gathered, most evacuees enjoyed their experiences at the Schools and some were genuinely sorry when the time came to return home. Sutton School began by billeting 188 boys in St Austell but by 1945 they had acquired premises which could be used as hostels. Elmsleigh at Par and Trelawney, a former isolation hospital on the outskirts of the town, together, accommodated 97 boys, with 42 still billeted.

Much was done to try to make the lives of the evacuees, who were so far from home, more enjoyable. In May 1942 a Ballroom Dancing class was begun by Miss Allen which met weekly from 6.30-7.30. The cost was 4d per head with tea in the Dining Hall for ½d. About 50 evacuees attended regularly and it is possible that one reason for its popularity was because it was the only time the girls were allowed, officially, to meet socially with the boys! In August 1941 Miss Bond arranged for 30 girls to go to Newquay County Girls' School for a holiday where the Headmistress, Miss Wood 'did everything possible to make them comfortable'.

The second major impact was on staffing. At least seven members of the Boys' School staff and several of the Girls' School joined the armed forces and they all went at more or less the same time. They were replaced by women teachers, some of whom were, for the first time, married teachers. All of these 'new' teachers were appointed on a temporary basis only and there was movement between the two Schools and other schools in the County, presumably to cater for the fluid nature of staffing. For instance, Miss Margaret Husband was appointed to the Boys' School in 1940 and in 1941 transferred to the Girls' when Mr Martin, who had been teaching History in both Schools, returned to the Boys'. Her sister, Joan, joined the Boys' in 1941 and 18 months later was transferred to Newquay Boys' as 'an emergency measure'. Most of these temporary appointments became stalwarts after the War, but there was much coming and going of some staff for short periods and the lack of permanency must have been difficult. Geoff Werry (1942-7) remembers that 'we had four or five different teachers for Latin and for French in the first two years.' In January 1941, a master from Shooters Hill School in London,

Above: *'Digging for Victory'. Boys digging up the lawn in front of the buildings to make a vegetable garden, November 1939 (Courtesy Cornish Guardian)*
Below: *One of the Girls' Harvest Camps 1943/4/5*

Mr JC Roberts, was sent by the LCC, to help to cope with the numbers of evacuees in the Boys' School. He certainly made an impression with his considerable contribution to the community both within the School and outside it – 'he was after all a Cornishman' (!), as Mr Barritt commented – and everyone was sorry to see him recalled to London in May 1943. The Girls' School had no chance of replacing their PE mistress, Miss Tucker, when she joined the WRNS in 1943, but some relief was at hand as Dartford PE College had been evacuated to Newquay and two third year students could come twice a week to help the other teachers who were filling the breach.

Outside the classroom, too, the War had its effects. The national 'Dig for Victory' campaign was responded to with the vigour one would expect after the First World War activities. The front of the Schools again became a garden and allotments were acquired in Tregonissey Road. Boys were 'persuaded', or volunteered to do the work under the able and practised eye of Mr 'Papa' Lodge. Saturdays and holidays saw a vast amount of labour rewarded with a wide variety of vegetables as well as many cwts of potatoes – in 1940, 25cwts of potatoes, 1½cwts of marrows, and much turnips, cabbages, brussels sprouts, savoys and broccoli – and it has been suggested that bad behaviour could have contributed to the War effort as the punishment was often garden duties! Besides supplementing the rations granted to the School Kitchen, occasionally there was enough to sell the surplus – in 1941 £7 worth of vegetables was sold. Seven hens were kept in a corner of the playing field next to Hillside Road, and Teresa Cronin (Ebbutt) used to help with the feeding of them and the collection of the eggs until, one night, some dogs broke in and killed them all. They were not replaced.

Beyond the school environment St Austell schoolchildren contributed to the War effort by working on farms during the various harvesting seasons. In the summer of 1941 the first boys' harvest camp was held at Duloe and until 1945 there were annual potato pickings at Penzance and harvest camps in the east of the county, together with ad hoc help to local farmers in term time as well as holidays. In May, 1942, for instance, 50 boys and two members of staff were in Penzance for two weeks and in 1944, a party of boys did three days farming work for Mr Kitto of Mevagissey. Ken Larcombe (1940-4) remembers the 1942 Penzance camp:

'We stayed in a converted barn, furnished with double-tier bunks in the dorms. There were dining areas and washing facilities. The day's work started at 8am which meant that the teachers who came to look after us, needed to rise early to prepare and cook breakfast. We were given a packed lunch consisting of rather thick slices of bread with some sort of filling. A national dried cocoa was provided for children during the War and made a most welcome drink. The weather was quite hot and we did not finish the day's work until late afternoon or early evening.......
The farm camp was accommodated on the Bolitho estate at Trengwainton. Expenses were paid by the Cornwall War Agricultural Committee and a small pocket money reward was given to each boy when returning to school.'

In 1943 the girls' first harvest camp, organised by Miss Margaret Husband, was at Quethiock with 30 girls and three members of staff, including Miss McVicar (later Mrs Clymo) and Miss Bond herself, in relays. It was deemed to be a great success and was followed by more at Duloe and Penzance. Miss Earl (later Mrs Richardson) gives us this account of her experience at a later camp:

'On our arrival we unloaded our packs in a large barn where we were to sleep. The next job was to dig a trench for the latrines. As I had done this for Girl Guide camps in the past, I volunteered, but when the spade came it was a Cornish one which I couldn't use, so local men did the digging. At night we frightened ourselves about rats, but none came. One day the farmer came and dumped twenty dead rabbits on the table for us to cook for the evening meal. There was a challenging look on his face. Admittedly they had been gutted but still had skins on. One VIth former lived on a farm herself and we tackled the job between us. She skinned eleven and I did nine. The farmer was most impressed! The girls came back from the potato fields very tired and hungry, so the rabbit meal was a success.'

There was also the more specialised work of collecting seaweed which was organised by Professor and Mrs Singer of Par. A jelly, agar-agar, which was valuable for medicinal research, was made from this particular, and relatively rare sea-

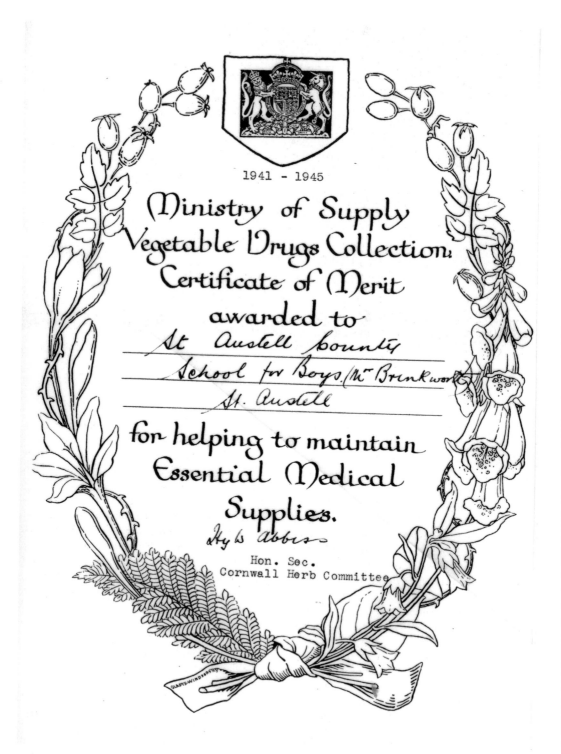

1941 - 1945

Ministry of Supply
Vegetable Drugs Collection:
Certificate of Merit
awarded to
St Austell County
School for Boys (Mr Brinkworth)
St. Austell

for helping to maintain
Essential Medical
Supplies.

Hy W Abbis

Hon. Sec.
Cornwall Herb Committee

Recognition of the boys' work in collecting, probably, seaweed

Collection of pots and pans in the Quad 1942. This was in response to government requests for metals, especially aluminium, to aid the War effort

weed which could be collected only at low Spring tides. It could be found at Vault beach, Gorran Haven and at Chapel Point, Mevagissey. From 1943 parties from both schools regularly went to collect it when the conditions were right.

The interiors of the Schools' buildings certainly took on a very different appearance. All windows were criss-crossed with tapes – a universal War time expedient to lessen the danger from flying glass, and from 1940 Morrison air raid shelters appeared in the class rooms and corridors on the ground floor of each building. These were supplemented with larger Anderson shelters in the playgrounds. Together these replaced the slit trenches dug in the playing field by the boys in 1939, in which all were supposed to sit when an air raid warning sounded. It was pointed out that, as most daylight 'raids' in Cornwall were stray individual planes looking for a likely target on the way home, it was not always wise for 400 or more children to be streaming in the open across the playing fields! Neither Mr Barritt nor Miss Bond was overwhelmingly pleased with the Morrison shelters which were 'always in the way of useful classroom

activity', and Miss Bond removed some bare metal laths which she considered to be 'a source of danger'. Mr Barritt was not impressed either with the Anderson shelters. Each held eight to twelve boys and the ventilation was so poor that he considered them to be a risk to the health of the boys after a very short time. Sand bags, buckets of water and hand pumps were spread around for action in the event of fire. Everyone had to carry a gas mask at all times. At first these were carried in square cardboard boxes with a string to carry them round the neck. There were occasional gas mask checks when the 'gas van' visited the Schools and the pupils had to be tested. Hilary Osborne (Crowle 1940-5) remembers 'the day we had to test our gas masks. A large van arrived at school which was full of tear gas. We had to be very brave and go into the van with our gas masks on and then remove them and feel the effect of the gas for a few moments. This made our eyes water and sting!'

However, there was the odd raid and Margaret Unitt (Rundell 1933-40) tells of 'several of us in June 1940, looking out of the window waiting for the bus to come to take us to Charlestown for

2nd St Austell Scout Troop May 1940

swimming. We saw a plane flying over the coast, and something drop from it. Then there was a bang and noise. We did not know until later, it was the first bombs dropped (in the district). They fell on the 'Grove' and killed a rabbit. There was no swimming that day!' There are other eye witness reports of bombing such as on the Goods Yard in 1943, but nothing any closer to the Schools.

Swimming at Charlestown did not survive for long. Par beach was mined to prevent invasion and many beaches were closed by barbed wire, with the approach roads blocked by tank traps. There were restrictions on travel which meant that sports fixtures, football, cricket, hockey and netball, were severely curtailed, with Sutton School, as they

were on the spot, being the Boys' most usual opponents. 1941 saw the last Sports Day until the end of the War, although the Boys' Magazine of 1943 notes that events were held during the last morning of term.

Other extra-curricular activities lapsed somewhat. The Boys' Magazine of 1943 looks forward to the return of Speech Days, the Reading Competition, the Literary and Debating Societies, the School Play, the 'Old Austellians' and an annual magazine. There were, however, a number of outside speakers who came, mostly but not exclusively, to talk about the War effort or their individual experiences. For instance, Lt Sharp DSC, RNVR had been a participant in the Dieppe Raid and

tance from the School. Expecting a modest company, over 60 girls were enthusiastic and two companies were formed. Activities were largely home based but did include collecting 21lbs of hips. There could be no camping and Freda Martin (Day 1941-5) remembers 'we only had one outing. This was a sausage sizzle to Helman Tor. It was cut short because it was discovered that Italian prisoners-of-war were working there.' A Junior Red Cross was also formed in the Girls' School, in 1942, by Miss Williams which obviously had its own appeal and relevance. First-Aid examinations were passed and money was raised for the Prisoners of War Fund. The St Austell Platoon of the Army Cadet Corps was founded in July 1942, and welcomed boys over fourteen years of age. Although not strictly connected to the Boys' School, all the NCOs were boys of the School who helped to keep it going when there were difficulties following the loss of army instructors.

Amazingly, during three Easter holidays Miss Saint and Miss Earl took parties of girls on walking trips to the Mendips (1943), the Cotswolds (1944) and the Brecon Beacons (1945) where they walked over 100 miles. Joy Averill (Walkey 1939-44) remembers: 'The best holiday in my life was a walking holiday in the Cotswolds with Miss Saint and Miss Earl in springtime. We stayed at Youth Hostels overnight and had two nights in Stratford, visiting the theatre both nights. I had the best meal of my life eating corned beef with fresh hot bread by the River Avon.'

National Savings Groups were supported in both Schools – the Boys' saving an exceptionally large £430 during Wings for Victory Week in 1943 – and the Spitfire Fund received donations; the Girls' sending £30 in the autumn of 1940. Collections were made of clothes and toys for evacuees and refugees, some of which was done during the summer holidays in the early years of the War, when the Schools remained open for voluntary attendance. In 1943 200 books and magazines were sent to the RN War Libraries together with contributions to the DCLI (Devon and Cornwall Light Infantry) POW Fund and the Prince of Wales Hospital in Plymouth.

These years did see some development in the welfare of school children. In February 1942 the distribution of school milk began. Each child was entitled to a third of a pint, daily. It was later that

Mlle Marconnet from the Free French Admiralty told of life in France under German occupation. In 1941 both Schools visited the Capitol to see a screening of *The Great Dictator* and there were a few dramatic performances by evacuated schools such as King's School's performance of Masefield's *Good Friday* at Crinnis in 1944.

The Scout Group continued to flourish, its numbers being swelled by evacuees from Bristol. At Easter 1941 they camped at Tregorrick Farm at Penrice, returning in August for ten days to help with the harvest; these camps continued throughout the War years. The Girl Guide Company was formed by Miss Margaret Husband in 1943, initially for evacuees and for girls living some dis-

The ceremony when Sutton High School said 'Thank you' to St Austell County Schools for their kindness and hospitality to the pupils and staff who were evacuated to St Austell. July 1946

small individual bottles were provided. At this time it had to be measured from the pint bottles into mugs and Teresa Cronin (Ebbutt) was very pleased that this was one of her tasks, as there was usually some left over! In May 1943 the Girls' School enjoyed its first ever dental inspection, which may have been by a mobile inspection team from Plymouth. Miss Bond noted that 100 of the 235 girls inspected, needed treatment. History does not record if they got it! In December 1944 the whole Boys' School had a medical inspection in the space of eight hours. Mr Barritt wondered how effective such an operation could have been and would it not have been better just to concentrate on the new entrants. The County continued to make appropriate grants for maintenance and travelling with the occasional free spectacles. In

the Girls' School the Watkins Memorial Fund provided a welcome £10 per year for worthy causes – this had been given by Mr Watkins in memory of his daughter, Phyllis who was Head Girl and died from meningitis in February 1940.

The staff who remained in St Austell made their contribution like the rest of the population. After Dunkirk, in 1940, the masters formed a branch of the LDV (Local Defence Volunteers), the forerunners of the Home Guard. They used to parade outside the School, but John Rockey remembers that a request was made asking if any fathers had a shot-gun they could borrow! From 1941 Mr Martin organised and ran an effective squadron of the ATC which was the largest in Cornwall. Fire watching in public buildings was an essential activity for civilians and all members of staff took part. Mrs Richardson remembers: 'Miss Bridgewater and I did one night and felt very nervous alone on the top corridor, scanning the sea and the skies. It was eerie and we didn't feel very confident about our ability to do anything with only a bucket of water and a stirrup pump.'

Public examinations continued to be taken with a total each year of about 60 from both Schools taking School Certificate and three or four from each School taking Higher. Both boys and girls gained an increasing number of places at universities, with WM (Mick) Lomer gaining an open scholarship to Queens', Cambridge, in 1944, and LW Martin, Mr Martin's son, the same to Christ's, Oxford, in 1945. While the girls' successes were not quite so spectacular Dorothy Jackson won an exhibition to Royal Holloway College, London in 1941 and Ruth Tregenza won a Ministry of Agriculture scholarship to Reading in 1944. Increasingly, entrants to teaching needed qualifications rather than the pupil-teacher route and twenty girls gained places at Teachers' Training Colleges during these years.

St Austell saw the arrival of troops from overseas at different times. In 1941, an Indian battalion, along with their mules, was based at Duporth and Tony Wilkinson (1942-7) remembers being given rides on the mules. In 1944, when southern Cornwall was overwhelmed with the US Army preparing for the invasion of France, the beaches were full of landing craft and the harbours with naval vessels. Ken Larcombe was given peanut butter, for the first time, by soldiers stationed near a harvest camp at Penzance.

Of course, perhaps above all, these years were particularly significant for the number of Old Boys who fought in the War. In 1943 a total of 328 were in the armed forces, including two chaplains, together with at least seven members of staff – this is the last date for which we have numbers. They served in all branches and in all arenas of the War, some being mentioned for particularly heroic deeds – Corporal H Hawke showed notable bravery in the retreat from Tobruk in 1942. Others were awarded service medals, such as JG Moore the DFM (Distinguished Flying Medal) in 1943, but most, from commissioned officers, to NCOs, to rank and file soldiers, sailors and airmen carried out their duties, whatever the difficulties. There were, sadly and inevitably, casualties. Thirty Old Boys were killed during this War. The first to fall, in July 1940, was Mr Lodge's only son, SP Lodge who was serving in the RAF, followed by WR Moyse, a Merchant Seaman in the same month. All their names were added to those who fell in the First World War, on the commemorative boards in what is now Poltair School.

6. POST WAR – GETTING BACK TO 'NORMAL'.

The War wrought great changes to the way of life, living and working and the Schools, too, were affected as they embarked on life post war.

The first major change was in personnel. Mr Barritt had retired in 1944 and it was he, together with Miss Bond, who, in the 1920s to 1940s, had been able to build so successfully on earlier foundations to establish the two Schools and pilot them through what must have been the difficult War years. Mr GH Brinkworth became the new Headmaster of the Boys' School bringing with him, probably a more rigorous academic approach – gone, for instance were the weekly Friday sing-songs so cherished by Mr Barritt, and in their place was Musical Appreciation, an introduction to classical music for the Vth and VIth Forms, apparently more appreciated by the Headmaster than the boys! Mr Lodge had also retired in 1944. He was the last of the 'founder' members of staff and Mr Barritt considered that it would be 'hard to imagine the School without him'. He had served as Senior Master from the beginning, becoming acting Headmaster when Mr Jenkinson went to War in 1915. Perhaps he is best remembered for his horticultural exploits during both World Wars. Mr Richardson took his place and worked with Mr Brinkworth until the two Schools amalgamated in 1962.

After 1945 there was another period of unease for the staff. War time appointments were temporary only, so that if and when teachers wanted to return to their posts from serving in the Forces, their jobs were secure. In fact only four men chose to reclaim their positions in St Austell which did not cause too much disruption, but there was much coming and going of part time staff. One who did not return was Major Symonds, the former Latin master, who became MP for Cambridge Town in the 1945 election. He was the first of two members of staff to sit in Parliament, the other was Robert Hicks, as MP for Bodmin, (later renamed SE Cornwall) from 1970 to 1997 with a few short breaks. The six women and five men who had been given only temporary contracts during the War, were made permanent in July 1946, along with Dr Wilson, who was appointed as Science

teacher in the Girls' School, from the WRAF. The real revolution for women teachers, of course, was that they were now able to retain their posts when married – a War time expedient now made permanent. Thus two members of staff whose positions were now secure were Miss Earl, who had married Mr Richardson, and Miss Scales, who had left the mixed School in 1929 to become Mrs Goode. Her husband, Group Captain HK Goode DSO, DFC, AFC, had been killed on active service, and she had returned to Cornwall.

The Butler Education Act of 1944 set out to give all children over the age of eleven specialist secondary education in Grammar, Secondary Modern or Technical Schools. The effect in Cornwall was by no means immediate because of the large numbers of scattered all-age village schools and the recognition by Cornwall Education Committee of the importance of such schools as the hub of their village communities. The two St Austell Schools were affected very little as children from a radius of some ten miles continued to take the annual LEA examination, awarding Special Places, soon to be known as the Scholarship. They proceeded automatically with at least partial exemption of fees, together with others who took the Schools' Entrance Examination and were liable for the payment of full fees of £3.5/- per term under twelve, rising to £4.6/- per term over twelve. There was still a reduction if three or more siblings were at school at the same time. Indeed, the situation remained so flexible that a request to the Governors for a girl, whose health was poor, be transferred back to Treverbyn School where her mother was a teacher was granted almost without question.

In July 1946 the LEA officially called its existing County Schools, County Grammar Schools but this was not adopted immediately. Indeed, Governors' Meetings were not listed as of St Austell Grammar Schools until July 1949, when a further result of the 1944 Education Act established a new governing body.

While not reaching the evacuee enhanced numbers of the War, both Schools continued to expand and in early 1949 the Boys' numbered 272 and the Girls' enjoyed an even greater rise to 288

Girls' School Staff 1948: Mrs Rundle, Mrs Goode, Miss Bridgewater, Dr Wilson, Mrs Richardson, Miss Tucker, Miss Chapman; Miss Husband, Mrs Babbage (later Mrs Clymo), Miss Lewis, Miss Bond, Miss Parry, Mrs Weaver, Miss Harris

– 50% in ten years. The Boys' School was staffed by the Headmaster and ten full time teachers, while the Girls' had fifteen full time, presumably employing fewer part time teachers.

The premises looked different after the air raid shelters were removed from the playgrounds in 1946 but they did not yet keep up with the increases in numbers. There are memories from the Girls' School of three classes being taught simultaneously in the Dining Hall before the 'huts' were built in the early 1950s. Governors' Minutes record frequent and repeated requests from both Heads for basic maintenance work to be done, such as internal/external painting, resurfacing of floors on the ground floor of the Boys' which were considered to be unsafe, to say nothing of heating in the Boys' cloakrooms and resurfacing of the netball/tennis courts. The General Inspection of the Boys' School in June 1949 highlighted a long list of premises deficiencies ranging from no gym, inadequate Science accommodation to lack of

washing facilities in the pavilion after games. But there was one innovation which must have made a considerable difference to the working of both Schools. In January 1945 the LEA agreed to the installation of electric lighting throughout.

The acquisition of equipment and teaching aids was a slow and difficult business. Indeed, much was the result of fund raising activities, such as a Sale of Work in November 1948, which enabled the Girls' School to purchase a duplicator for £50 and another 'wireless' for £20. Sometimes they received welcome gifts. Mrs Sellick, a new Governor in 1949, gave a portable gramophone.

School dinners continued to flourish with meals costing 5d. At Speech Day in December 1945, Miss Bond reported that the Kitchen, built to cater for 200 children, somehow fed 270. She remarked: 'It reminds one of the feeding of the 5,000, but that wasn't a hot dinner!' It was, of course, still a period of food rationing, at times more stringent than during the actual War, and

Girls' Winter Uniform 1947-8: Form VA with Miss Lewis

Mrs Beable's efforts were appreciated by most. She left in 1947 when her husband retired as caretaker and Mrs Allen succeeded her. She, too, won praise, apart from moans about spam and corned beef. Eating school dinner continued to be one of the few occasions when all boys and girls could socialise officially. Personal memories of this period differ. Trevor Bassett (1945-51) remembers that they sat in year order and moved up each year. The nearer they got to the prefect at the end serving the food, the larger the portions. Another young man reports that the girls always had first choice and always got more than the boys, certainly until the IIIrd Year! While the Inspectors of 1949 thought the arrangement to be a good one, 'it was too fast for real social development'!

Uniform was another casualty of the War. Clothing coupons made it impossible to expect all pupils to conform completely and the girls, especially, wore what they had as long as it was 'acceptable'. As rationing restrictions eased, so the boys resumed their purple blazers – only purple caps had been compulsory – and the girls their bottle green with white blouses in the winter and green checked cotton dresses in the summer.

There was, however, very little amendment to the curriculum with both Schools continuing to teach a broadly academic programme. There was significant expansion of the VIth Form – there were twenty in the Boys' School in 1949 and 30 in the Girls' in 1947. Generally they were able to acquire the qualifications they needed, but there was one notable exception. David Blight (1941-48) wanted to read Agriculture at Reading University where a Cornwall County Council Scholarship was available for the sons of farmers. The requirement was Chemistry, Physics, Botany and Zoology. Botany and Zoology were not available at the Boys' School. After a year of Botany with Miss Saint in the Girls' School, Mr Brinkworth arranged for him to be taught both at Truro Girls', Miss Saint having left St Austell. Even then it was not plain

Girls' Summer Uniform 1948: Form IB with Miss Parry, Miss Bond and Mrs Julian

sailing as he encountered, along with many of his contemporaries, the problem of university departments being overwhelmed by applicants from the Forces. Prospective students often had to spend a third year in the VIth Form. The libraries in both Schools continued to develop gradually with more space allocated to them, together with extra furniture such as shelving. Many old students made gifts of books when they left to go to university and this certainly helped to swell the stock.

The punishment/reward system remained as it had been for many years. Good work and achievement were rewarded with stars, and unacceptable behaviour and poor work received the dreaded stripe. At the end of each term a tally was calculated which, together with success of House teams on the sports field, contributed towards the competitive achievement of the award of best House. More heinous misdemeanours by the boys resulted in corporal punishment, often performed in public. There are memories of one young man who received the treatment for relieving himself in a fellow's boot.

Both Schools continued to enjoy success both at School Certificate and Higher. In 1945, 26 of 34 boys were successful at School Certificate as were 23 of 25 girls. At Higher all six boys who entered passed, together with four of the seven girls. These numbers were more or less sustained for the rest of the 1940s, with corresponding success for entry to Higher Education. Between 1946-50, fourteen boys who achieved Higher proceeded to university with five County Scholarships and two Open or closed awards including Geoff Lomer (1942-50), who followed his brothers with an Open Exhibition in Natural Sciences at Queens' College, Cambridge. Seven girls proceeded to university during this time, including, in 1949 Margaret Haley (1941-9) to read History at Somerville College, Oxford, but an increasing number – 36 – were entering Teachers' Training Colleges. Some who had embarked on a

Girls' VIth Form Play about 1948: Ann Brinkworth, Mary Lomer, Margaret Brinkworth (courtesy Mary Clayton)

teaching career by the pupil teacher route before the War, were able to enjoy a year of 'official' training as mature students. Many endured a delayed start because of the 'Emergency Training' scheme which, again, filled colleges with those returning from the Forces. As for many years, leavers from both Schools gained positions in the civil service, banks, local businesses, many of which were connected with the clay industry, and every sort of clerical/professional trainee post.

Old Boys' successes in the wider world began to have an impact on the boys. AJ Pascoe was living and working in Rome and offered free hospitality to any two boys nominated by the Headmaster. History does not record how many boys were able to take advantage of this splendid offer. In 1948, Mrs B Easterbrook of Pasadena, California began an annual gift of 50 Roget's Thesaurus to pupils of both Schools, in memory of her husband, William, who had spent his boyhood in St Austell before emigrating. Anne Treneer, by now a celebrated author after the publication of *Schoolhouse in the Wind* in 1944, was the guest speaker at the Girls'

Speech Day in 1949.

The curriculum continued to be enhanced by a succession of outside speakers to both Schools, covering a wide range of subjects. Some, inevitably, referred back to the War with, for instance, Major Symonds, in 1945, relating his experiences. Others highlighted current world problems such as *Leprosy Relief in Nigeria*, in 1949, and, for the first time, speakers addressed the question of careers. In 1946 the Labour Exchange gave general advice on Careers, and in 1948 *Agriculture as a Career* was given to the boys. Besides talks, there was an increasing number of cultural presentations including piano recitals, the Compass Players presenting *Drama through the Ages* and a consideration of Rembrandt. These were not innovations but a building on former practices.

Extra curricular activities continued to thrive. The Debating Society gave the boys food for thought, there now being a Junior branch as well as the Senior. The latter considered such weighty contemporary issues as: 'That compulsory National Service should become a permanent fea-

Easter 1948: Lunch during a hike at Ambleside in the Lake District
(courtesy Mary Clayton)

ture in our national life' and: 'That nationalisation decreases the freedom of the individual', both of which were carried. The Juniors put their minds to issues of immediate concern to them such as: 'That boys who stay to School dinner should give up their meat coupons', which lost, and: 'That homework should be abolished' which, unsurprisingly, was carried!

1946 saw the welcome return of the pre-war Reading Competition in the Boys' School, and music continued to be an important part of the lives of both Schools. The Girls' enjoyed their, by now traditional, success at County Music Festivals, the choir winning the County Shield in 1948, and, from December 1948, contributed to the newly formed St Austell Music Festival. The Boys' took part in the County Music Festival in 1949 – the first time since 1940. Folk Dancing became an important activity in the Girls' School, meeting for practice once a week, with annual visits to the County Festival held at different venues. In June 1949, for instance, Miss Husband took 80 girls to Penzance.

There is little detailed record of dramatic performances by either School during this period, although the 1949 Inspection Report of the Boys' School says there was a public performance every two years. Governors' Minutes report that the Boys' School Play of 1948 was a great success and raised £27, but they do not say which play was performed. The VIth Form of the Girls' School put on annual plays at Christmas but, again, there are no details recorded. The Old Austellians continued to put on productions such as *The Admirable Crichton* by JM Barrie in 1949. Expeditions continued to be made to significant films such as both Schools seeing Olivier's *Henry V* in October 1945 – a film which impinged upon the post war psyche – I, too, was taken to see that film in Bristol at about the same time!

The Boys' held annual Carol Services in St Johns, with the collection being given to charity, and the Rededication Service, initiated by Mr Brinkworth in 1945, became another annual event in the Spring in the Parish Church.

While the Boys' School Magazine resumed in

Hockey 1st XI 1948-9: J Aldred, A Warnes, Mrs Richardson, S May, S McAuliffe, J Whetter;
P Wall, J Trethewey, J Oliver, B Vivian (Capt), M Lomer (V Capt), M Brinkworth

1946, the first Girls' School edition since 1939, was in 1949 prefaced by Miss Bond's editorial: 'Our School Magazine was a War casualty – not mortally wounded but Reported Missing – but now completely recovered we hope, here it is again reporting for duty.'

The girls continued their expeditions 'up country' as well as more pioneering work in Europe. For instance, in July 1947 there was a ten day Geography Expedition to Snowdonia with Mrs Richardson and Miss Harry, and the following Easter to the Lake District with Dr Wilson and Miss Harry. In April 1950, an expedition took off for a week in Paris, again with Dr Wilson and Miss Harry. There is no record of the boys travelling far afield apart from some scouts going to the 6th World Jamboree in France in August 1947. Their activities were enjoyed closer to home with potato picking on local farms – to aid the food distribution difficulties – and more seaweed gathering for medical purposes.

Sporting activities, of course, continued to be pursued but not with the outstanding team successes of former years – perhaps the rest of the county was beginning to catch us up! However, there were individual successes. In 1945 two girls, Mary Dorman and Madeline Ferris, were the first from St Austell to be selected to play hockey for Cornwall and, in 1947, four boys, who were cadets in the 1225 ATC Squadron, took part in the ATC National Championships at White City in London. David Michael followed up his success of winning the Junior Mile in 1946 by coming second in the Senior Mile which 'he lost by inches'. Derek Tremayne won the 100 and 220 yards, Alf Bowyer the Long Jump and Geoffrey Werry was third in the 880 yards – quite an achievement for a relatively small Cornish Grammar School. Athletics matches between the Boys' School and Sutton High School were an annual feature – St Austell won for the first time in 1946 – as were Sports Days for each School. Swimming at Charlestown occurred spasmodically during the summer term, with annual Swimming Sports Days in the Girls' School at least. There are reports of various matches in different disciplines against the Staff,

Football 1st XI 1949-50: DC Palmer (Capt), D Haley (V Capt), J Ball, G Mannell, N Dale, S Benallick, GC Kent, O Hore, J Bettey, D Bowyer, K Andrew, M Jacob, S May

sometimes single sex, sometimes mixed.

Both the Army Cadet Corps and the ATC pursued peace time activities besides basic military training; the ATC was particularly active and effective in encouraging and sponsoring athletics. Both continued their annual summer camps with the ATC being able to arrange for flying experience. There were, however, constant wranglings about the status of the ATC hut in the Boys' School grounds. In 1946 the arrangement was that it would be rent free with the School having use of it, appropriately, and the LEA paying for heating and lighting. In 1949 a new problem appeared with the UDC demanding the payment of rates. On that occasion the ATC was deemed to be responsible for the payment but there were further 'discussions' with the UDC about the level of the rates. The 2nd St Austell County School Scout Troop celebrated its tenth anniversary in 1946, although its headquarters were still in the Drill Hall in Mount Charles. Scouts continued to contribute to local, national and international initiatives as well as pursuing their individual

quests for tests and badges. By 1949 the 2nd St Austell Girl Guide Company had five flourishing patrols, although clothes rationing hit hard and led to an appeal for cast off uniforms. They, too, were enjoying their quest for badges with three Guides working towards their 1st Class Badge. They also helped to man stalls at fetes and put on displays of their work for parents. They undertook hiking expeditions in mid Cornwall especially to Carworgie, the home of their Captain, Miss Husband, at St Columb Road. They won the Kirkby Shield for the South Cornwall Division, and, in 1949, it was reported, were working towards the County Bolitho Shield.

The War time innovation, initially for the evacuees, of the weekly Old Time Dancing Class was run now by Miss Bridgewater and Miss Tucker. This was another occasion when Vth and VIth Form boys and girls were given official blessings to mingle. It was much appreciated by the members who attended and David Michael (1941-47) considers that 'they taught us skills and attitudes and made social events much more civilised and much

2nd St Austell Guides preparing for their 1st Class about 1947: Mary Lomer and Margaret Brinkworth (courtesy Mary Clayton)

more enjoyable'. End of term parties were enjoyed by all concerned, as indeed were the House parties which were also an end of term feature, with the Boys' often indulging in fancy dress affairs.

While there was still a measure of financial support for pupils whose families needed it, the criteria appear to have been altered by the LEA, by 1946. In the post war period grants were made for maintenance and clothing, but far fewer than previously. For instance, in the summer of 1947, two girls received maintenance awards of £12, and three for clothing, ranging from £1.10/- to £4.13/-, while for 1947/8, five boys received maintenance from £5-£12 and three clothing at £10. The Sydney Hancock Scholarship, established in memory of a founding Governor, Mr HS Hancock, 1908-25, was still in funds – in 1947 with £200 in 3½% War Stock and £46.2/7d in credit. Annual awards were made to students at universities, but, in 1948, Governor involvement was limited to recommendations as the administration was taken over by the FE sub committee of the Education Committee. A limited number of

County Scholarships for some university students continued to be awarded.

There was a delay, similar to that in 1918, in setting up the memorial boards to those 30 Old Boys who had been killed in the War. While the memorial windows to the First World War casualties, which had been removed for safe keeping during the War, were restored almost immediately in November 1945 by Mr Lodge, it was not until Armistice Day 1948 that the memorial boards to the casualties of both Wars were dedicated by Mr Barritt, the previous Headmaster. Good quality wood was in such short supply that Mr May, the Woodwork master in charge of producing the new boards, is said to have remarked that it would have been disastrous had a mistake been made. The quality is such that they are still in good shape in their home for nearly sixty years.

The winter of 1947 was a particularly severe one with large falls of snow in January and February. There were fuel shortages, in this time of austerity, and in February Years I-IV were sent home when the coke supply failed, and with it the

Free milk in the Quad late 1940s

Boys' School Prefects 1945 including: PR Walters, ID Shaw, MB Lean, WEJ Neal, J Cloke, AM Jane, TC Common, RM Kendall

central heating. Vth and VIth formers were taught around a few oil stoves – the Cornish Guardian referring to the girls as 'shivering Amazons'! One result of this was that in the summer of 1947, the Clerk to the Governors was authorised to buy fuel early for the following winter in case fuel supplies should be difficult again. There were also difficulties with the distribution of food supplies. The Cornish Guardian reports on December 19th, 1946 that each pupil at the County Schools had been asked to bring two potatoes to school on December 18th because of a severe shortage. History does not record how many were brought, but Molly Richards (Light) certainly remembers the incident.

The Brewery continued to make an impact on all those who worked in the Schools' buildings. W Bate (1944-9) remembers that 'I vowed I would never drink beer after smelling the Brewery on a damp, foggy day – but that was soon forgotten!' Lorraine Castle (Roberts 1947-51) also remembers that the smell made them 'all feel nauseated' when having to play hockey immediately before

the dinner hour when they were all hungry.

Transport problems had not been resolved satisfactorily and there were frequent references in Governors' Minutes to difficulties encountered by pupils on buses. St Dennis and Gorran Haven appear to be the most affected and in 1949 the 22 pupils from Gorran Haven were not always able even to get on the bus, and when they did, it was very overcrowded. The situation from St Dennis was similar. The Area Traffic Superintendant of Western National was asked to ensure that all children were able to travel. There is no record of a reply.

There were significant Staff resignations towards the end of this period. Mr Hobba, a strict disciplinarian who 'inspired terror in most of us', according to Kenneth Sweet (1944-9), but who was completely overcome when his form, VA, presented him with a matching cigarette case and lighter when he left in 1949. He had been a pupil at the Mixed County School in its earliest years, one of the 101 in September 1908. Miss Lewis, too, left in 1949 because of ill health, having joined

Girls' School Prefects 1948 including: C Axford, D Hore, J Trethewey, M Brinkworth, M Lomer, J Robins, B Hawke, A Wakeham

the Mixed School in May 1916, teaching general subjects until in 1928 she gained an external degree in French. Her starting salary was £100pa, as was Miss Parry's who also began her long teaching career in 1916 and retired in 1950 after 34 years of service. Perhaps her most significant contribution was to Music and particularly to the Mixed and then Girls' Choirs. Mr May, 'Benchy May', sadly died early in 1950, having given sixteen years to attempting to improve boys' woodworking skills.

However, the Summer of 1950 really was the end of the beginning when Miss Bond retired. She had served the Schools for 28 years, twelve as Senior Mistress in the Mixed School and sixteen as Headmistress of the Girls'. When, early in the year she said she would be retiring, Governors' minutes reported as follows: 'After the Governors present had personally expressed their appreciation of Miss Bond's excellent work and of her influence for good on the many pupils who have passed through the Schools, it was unanimously resolved to place on record the

Governors' thanks and appreciation of her loyal and devoted service and to wish her a long and happy retirement.' She was a much respected and much loved Headmistress who believed that all children had considerable potential and who had the happy knack of persuading many of them to realise that potential. Her Speech Day speeches always had an educational message, but her humour also managed to enliven the proceedings. Apparently she had not an ounce of pomposity and Miss Bridgewater remembers the occasion when, dressed as a parlour maid and ready to go to the Hall for an end of term party, she opened the door to a Book Traveller and dealt with him with complete aplomb. At another time she allowed a Ist former to pin 'April Fool' on her back before going to take Assembly and, what's more, checked that the said small child had received the bar of chocolate she had been promised by the VIth former! Dr Wilson, too, recalls that her reply to an official enquiry as to where the girls swam, was to write on the form: 'in the Atlantic'.

Her resignation raised the question of the

future of the two Schools and Mr Brinkworth suggested to a Governors' Meeting that they should merge, in spite of Chairman, Mr EB Vian's proposal in 1945 'to reserve the present County Schools' buildings at St Austell for girls and to build another one for boys'. This suggestion was rejected as it was felt that it would 'serve no useful purpose bearing in mind the dubious educational advantages, the reaction of both sets of staff and the existing accommodation'. Thus, in 1950, Miss FLE Camous was appointed as the second Headmistress of the Girls' School, beginning a new era in the history of the Schools.

We can imagine that the rendering of *Red River Valley* at the end of the summer term was even more fervent than usual. This most unlikely of 'school songs' was first aired as part of Mr Barritt's Friday afternoon sing-songs and was adopted by the Girls' School at the start of their existence in 1933 and sung at the end of each term. This tradition was maintained, often in spite of opposition, until the early 1960s. It is still fondly remembered by Old Girls and sung at many a reunion.

7. The Iron Curtain Descends   1950-62

In 1950 Mr Brinkworth had been in post for six years and, while relations with Miss Bond were cordial, there was not the closeness which there had been when Barritt/Bond reigned supreme. The atmosphere was to become decidedly less cordial with the arrival of Miss Camous in September 1950. She had been educated in a girls' school, taught in three and been headmistress of three. She was devoted to the education of girls in a single sex establishment, and determined to promote their academic and moral development at all costs. Particularly, this meant the complete segregation from boys during school time, and this was supposed to be sustained even on the bus on the way to school! This appeared to match Mr Brinkworth's approach during the '50s and relations between the two Schools were cool and formal with joint activity extremely limited and strictly monitored.

The numbers of the pupils, post the 1944 Education Act, continued to rise steadily. In 1950 there were 272 in the Boys' School and 315 in the Girls'. Until 1962 the Girls' School continued to be larger than the Boys' with 446 girls and 365 boys in 1961, just before amalgamation. Approximately 25% of the pupils from 25 LEA primary schools were admitted each year, together with a few from private schools such as the Lawn School in St Austell and Roselyon in Par. Frances Smith (Tresize 1959-66) was somewhat in awe of those from the Lawn School who had already done French – it did not last long! In 1962 there was a VIth Form of 75 in the Girls' School and, in 1959, the latest statistic available, some 38 boys, plus a Vth Remove of thirteen, who returned to re-take subjects in which they had not been successful.

The Girls' School, particularly, suffered severe problems of overcrowding. The School had been

'The Shack' erected as a temporary class room in the 1920s, it became the Boys' School Music Room and was finally demolished in 1960

built in 1933, for 151 pupils and the numbers had more than doubled with no extra accommodation. In 1950 it was Miss Camous's first request to rectify the situation, and it was to be her lasting and most vociferous demand to the LEA. Gradually both Schools had new buildings. In 1953 the Girls' had what was known, not very imaginatively, as New Block I, housing a Biology Laboratory and a form room, to be followed, in 1956, by New Block II with a Geography Room and an Art Room. They were substantial, block built, permanent buildings, each with two rooms. Small cloakrooms between the rooms in each were necessary as it was the beginning of a period when both staff and pupils had to run, in the rain, to outside classrooms. Later the Boys' had a new hut which became the Music Room, the old one described by Phil King (1959-65) as 'a wooden shack' – can this

By 1962 the Girls' School had a room dedicated to being a Library. A member of staff, Mrs Hanssens, acted as Librarian and VIth formers as Library Prefects

have anything to do with the music master, Mr Alan Hutt being known as 'Shack'? In 1959, the Girls' acquired use of a further classroom when the Lower Old Kitchen, in the middle of the Boys' playground, became available. It is not known what the administrative arrangements were but the boys lost a potential Art Room, and the girls had to be shepherded very carefully to and fro, with absolutely no communication between girls and boys, or even between members of staff! In September 1958, a new, purpose built Woodwork Room was opened, and by 1960 both Schools were using the old Carclaze Infants' School, a fairly far off outpost, as an Art Room. This was not an entirely satisfactory arrangement, but it was the best available. It was a time when children were trusted to walk, in this instance unaccompanied, to their Art lessons, and to arrive on time, which, generally, they did.

Apart from subjects requiring specialist rooms such as laboratories, until 1958 boys remained in their form rooms and the staff moved. Thereafter, boys were constantly on the move. Lauraine Sadlier (Pascoe 1953-8) also remembers, 'moving to different classrooms for various lessons, the Chemistry Lab., the Library and Latin was something completely alien.' The sheer size of the school and the maze of corridors' was an initial shock to many. Penny Trethewey (1958-64) had been told, by her cousin Elizabeth Watts, of the stairs which had 'glittery bits on the edges, perhaps it was granite chippings, but I certainly remember them sparkling in the sun.' At a time when primary schools did not have uniforms, a further culture shock was seeing all the pupils wearing uniform and teachers wearing gowns. 'The sight of masters wearing black gowns created quite an impression and certainly earned a degree of respect' from Phil King (1959-65).

Gradually the grounds were restored to their pre-war condition with the trenches in the Boys' playground being filled in properly in 1953. Also in 1953, to mark the Coronation, a lily pond was created in front of the Boys' School, described by two members of Form III, thus:

The Gold Fish Pond

While all the boys were working hard,
One fine and sunny morn,
The caretaker and groundsman
Were digging up the lawn.

Now all the boys were curious
To what this digging meant,
So they pestered Mr Body,
To find out his intent.

At last the reason was found out;
A pond it was to be,
A coronation souvenir,
For everyone to see.

The digging soon was finished with,
And then to our delight
The earth was covered with cement,
Which made it watertight.

It soon was filled with H2O,
'To cleanse it', so 'twas said,
And when we saw it later on,
The water had turned red.

And when the pond was clean once more,
And filled with water clear,
Mr Julian brought some lily plants,
To flower every year.

For a surprise, the generous men,
Who wear the old school tie,
Presented an electric fount,
Which squirts the water high.

Now to complete this lovely pond,
As far as I can tell,
Gold fish and scavengers were bought,
Shubunkin fish as well.

When people come to this, our school,
The gold fish pond they see,
And know this school is still as good,
As it was wont to be.

WR Fitton and C Pepper

These were the major building developments but General Inspections of the Girls' School in 1956 and the Boys' in 1959, highlighted many other inadequacies, such as no medical rooms – sick girls were placed on a couch in the corridor, behind screens – no VIth Form rooms and a lack of hot water in the cloakrooms of both pupils and staff. Very few of these deficiencies were tackled before 1962. The shared use of the Hall, criticised in 1956, was, to some extent, resolved in 1959 when the Dining Hall was adapted for PE for the Girls', with wall bars, but no ropes, and a small store for equipment. The Girls' also used the Dining Hall for assemblies, with form room prayers on some days of the week, with the Boys' having sole use of the Hall. For Speech Days and public presentations, there continued to be shared use.

The Dining Hall and Kitchen, built in 1932 to provide a maximum of 200 meals daily, could no longer serve a sufficient number of meals at one sitting and, in 1955, boys and girls ate at separate sessions. The girls ate first, followed by the boys. This meant that the one regular, communal activity where boys and girls could mix, came to an end. The serving of the food, as before, was prefect led. The canteen staff delivered it to each table in large metal containers, and a prefect divided it and distributed it to each of the eight or ten at the table. Memories of the quality are generally good – 'Very filling and good, but not exciting', says Russell Semmens (1959-65), but there is some dispute about the custard. Frances Smith (Tresize 1959-66) remembers 'wonderful custard', an opinion shared by Richard Turner (1956-63), while Margaret Hodge (Matthews 1957-62) says that the regular steamed pudding was served with 'watery custard'. Yet again, Caroline Nash (Rowe 1957-64) remembers 'different coloured custards – blue, pink, yellow!' Grace was said by a member of staff, before each sitting could begin.

As numbers increased so, too, did the staff expand, creating different problems as the Staff Rooms were too small. In 1956 the Girls' School enjoyed a Staff of eighteen full time members, fifteen of whom were graduates with three specialists in practical subjects – Domestic Science, Art and PE – with two part time teachers and a French assistant. In 1961, for the first time, a German assistant, Fraulein Strocka, joined the staff – a

Girls' School Staff 1961-2 which had expanded to a total of 27. **Back Row:** *myself, Miss Grose, Miss Olds, Miss Whitehead, Mr Bending, Miss Newbould, Mrs Steward, Mrs Hanssens.* **Middle Row:** *Dr Matthews, Miss Stone, Miss Alford, Miss Bowly, Mrs Stirling, Miss Spurr, Miss Tregunna, Mrs Davey, Miss Tyzzer, Miss Blair.* **Front Row:** *Fraulein Strocka, Dr Wilson, Mrs Richardson, Miss Husband, Miss Camous, Mrs Clymo, Miss Bridgewater, Mrs Weaver, Mmlle Lauret*

great achievement as the Ministry of Education recognised the development of the teaching of Languages. In 1959, Mr Brinkworth was assisted by fifteen full time teachers of whom, as in the Girls' School, all but three were graduates, and three part time teachers in Art and Handicraft. The Inspectors did not consider the staffing in either School to be over-generous. The management of the Boys' School remained the same throughout this period, with Mr Richardson acting as deputy to Mr Brinkworth, and, when he was ill during 1959, Mr Martin filled the position. In the Girls' School Mrs Goode was the deputy to Miss Camous until she retired in 1957 when Miss Margaret Husband succeeded her. There was a regular turn-over of staff throughout the period with 1956 and 1957 seeing a particularly large change in the Girls' School, with five new members of staff in 1956, including Miss Tyzzer, the first Old Girl to be appointed, and a further seven, including me, in 1957, representing a two thirds turn over in two years. The Boys' School saw the departure of several stalwarts from the early days

including Mr Holland (1927-52) who sadly died, and the retirement of Mr Julian (1930-56). Mr T Crabb became the second Old Boy to be appointed as a full time member of staff and this period also saw the appointment of masters who were to become fixtures in both the Mixed School and later the Sixth Form College – Messrs A Hutt, FF Farnham-Flower, J Wearing, K Hunter and RJ Lincoln. In 1957 both Schools appointed full time laboratory assistants, Mrs Davis in the Boys' and Mrs Bennett (later Mrs Dove) in the Girls'. In 1952 each School, at last, enjoyed the services of a full time clerical assistant when Miss Daniel's position in the Girls' School was made permanent with Mrs Lindsley and later Miss M Davey, as full time in the Boys' School. No doubt their task was made rather easier when, in 1954, at last after much pressure from the Heads, each School had its own telephone.

There were considerable changes, too, in the pay structure for teachers. The national system, known as the Burnham award, was negotiated between the government, the employers who were the LEAs, and the teaching unions. In 1951, when the average basic rate of pay was approximately £500pa posts of special responsibility were awarded, above the basic rate. In the Girls' School Mrs Goode, the Senior Mistress, received an extra £80 pa and there were a further four awards, while Mr Richardson of the Boys' School received £90, there being a further five awards. The following year Mrs Goode received £95, with six further awards ranging from £40-£65, and Mr Richardson remained at £90 with the same further number and rates as the Girls'. In 1957 there was the further development of Departmental Headships, when members of staff were rewarded for the organisation and running of their subjects. The Girls' had seven such awards ranging from £100-£220, and the Boys' seven, from £125-£225. Beside these salary additions other members of staff were given awards for work considered to be above the norm, perhaps running a small department, or significant VIth Form teaching or contribution to extra curricular activity. There were ten such posts in the Girls' of £60pa each, and six in the Boys' of £75. Equal pay for men and women was achieved over a seven year period, beginning in the mid 1950s, with the gap between men's and women's pay being eroded by $1/7^{th}$ each year.

Maternity leave provided a new problem for governing bodies. When married women were not employed, the issue did not arise. However, in 1959, Dr Matthews applied for maternity leave and this was granted but, there was a stern addendum that, in future, 'domestic matters were not to interfere with her teaching'! The situation was clarified in Cornwall County Council's 1961 'Conditions of Service of Primary and Secondary School Teachers' which laid down the length of the leave and the rather complicated arrangements concerning pay.

The curriculum did not change significantly in either School with the emphasis still on the academic route. However, by 1959 the Boys' curriculum had been divided into academic subjects, where boys were prepared for public examinations, and non-academic where they were not – Religious Instruction, Art, Music, Handicraft and PE. Mr Alan Hutt tells us that Mr Brinkworth did not favour these subjects being taken at O/A levels because the constraints of the syllabus made the teaching too narrow. The girls had opportunities

to take practical subjects for public examinations, including Cookery, Needlework, Music and Art, as well as Religious Knowledge, but were usually limited to Biology or General Science, while all the boys could take Physics and Chemistry. The VIth Forms followed a broadly Arts or Science programme with, in both Schools, University or Teacher Training College entrance being the main objective. The Girls' had a third option which was a General curriculum, including Domestic Science and academic subjects, aiming to prepare girls for careers such as nursing, secretarial training and the Civil Service.

There was a small expansion of the curriculum of both schools, when, in the summer of 1962, the lower forms enjoyed swimming lessons, on one morning per week, at what was then called the Riviera Club at Carlyon Bay, arranged by the LEA. Apparently Mr Brinkworth never let a Speech Day go by without reference to the fact that St Austell had no indoor swimming pool, and this was not to be resolved for many years. String classes began in 1959 with the teaching of woodwind instruments also making a hesitant start in 1960. In the Girls' School, because of the high cost of the instruments only two girls could benefit, one on the flute and the other on the clarinet, but at least it was a beginning.

Success at School Certificate, and after 1951, General Certificate of Education (GCE), reflected the increasing numbers, both at Ordinary Level and Advanced. In 1951, five boys achieved 16 passes at Advanced Level, and in 1962, 25 boys achieved 46 passes, with five being unsuccessful. Similarly, in 1951, four girls achieved fourteen passes at Advanced Level while in 1962, 24 achieved 49 passes with three being unsuccessful. At this stage, nationally, only a very small proportion of the school population took A Levels as very few careers demanded an A Level qualification, and of these, most aimed at university or specific professional training – neither teacher training nor nursing for instance, at this stage, demanded A Level qualification. In 1951, 35 girls and 24 boys achieved at least three subjects at Ordinary Level at the end of their Vth year, and this had risen to 57 and 35, respectively, by 1962. GCE was different from School Certificate in that it was possible to take a single subject, resulting in a pass or fail, rather than having to pass a group of subjects resulting in gaining a Certificate, or not.

While we have no detailed statistics for the Boys' School, during this period 48 boys gained State Scholarships or County Awards and we can assume that there was a steady flow to university, including DM Hobba's Open Exhibition to Cambridge to read History in 1952. Raymond Trudgian (1948-55) was another of those who progressed to Cambridge, to read Theology, with memories of Mr Rowe's inspiring him in Classical Greek as well as Latin. In 1959 Clive Mitchell won an RAF Scholarship to Cranwell as well as a State Scholarship. Of the girls, 43 went on to university with Mary Lomer winning an Open Exhibition to read History at Oxford in 1951 and her cousin, Jennifer, the Winifred Holtby Exhibition in Physics also at Oxford the following year, along with June Bull to read Natural Sciences at Cambridge. In 1957 Grace Wilkinson, became the first St Austell girl to read Medicine, at London University, followed by Heather Willcox. Four years later, Marlene Behennah gained a place at Oxford to read for the same degree. 109 girls undertook teacher training, and 48 embarked on a variety of nursing training schemes, both specific such as children's and orthopaedic, and general. Professional training, which had not been readily available before, attracted an increasing number of girls. Dawn Harris went to the Royal College of Music at Manchester in 1955, Ann Nicholls undertook training for Occupational Therapy in 1957, Heather George began a Physiotherapy course in 1959, Brenda May went to Bristol General Hospital in 1961 to train for a career in Radiography and, in 1962, Heather Best embarked on a career in Osteopathy and Jacqueline Reeves in Speech Therapy. An increasing number, too, were taking Secretarial Courses, both at Cornwall Technical College in Camborne, and out of the County, many at the London College of Secretaries. This illustrates the broadening of career options for girls and the increasing availability of careers information in the 1950s, in co-operation with the Ministry of Labour, as well as the determination of St Austell girls to make the most of these opportunities.

Information on boys' careers was recorded differently but we do know that 30 boys embarked on Services careers including entry to Cranwell and Welbeck Colleges, while seventeen left the VIth Form for their National Service before starting a career. Between 1956 and 1959, ten boys proceeded to Colleges of Further Education and 36 took up technical apprenticeships. A number of boys was always recruited by Cable and Wireless at Porthcurno, Devonport Dockyard, the Post Office and Camborne School of Mines. The Civil Service, both nationally and in Cornwall, continued to be a major source of employment for both boys and girls, together with St Austell Brewery and other local firms connected to the clay industry, banks and family businesses.

Funding for Higher Education became much more accessible with State Scholarships being introduced in 1949. These were more difficult to achieve, requiring extra examination papers to be taken, and were designed to supplement the University Scholarships and Exhibitions awarded by LEAs. Specialist professional training was funded largely by the awarding bodies, making aspirations to such careers much more realistic.

The Sydney Hancock Scholarship ceased to be of much practical value during the 1950s, as any award made led to a reduction in the national or LEA grant. It was a similar situation with the Fifield Bequest. Originally a sum of money, £1,000, was invested in memory of Salome Hocking, a member of a well known St Stephen family, the income from which was administered by the LEA to help to fund the education of any deserving girl of the parish. It had been revived in 1947, after being in abeyance for several years, and in 1948 and 1949, two girls had been assisted at their Teacher Training Colleges. In 1950 it was resolved that as grants were a better option for girls at university and training college, it would be preferable if the Fund were administered by the Headmistress and Governors and allocated to help girls from St Stephens, over the age of sixteen, while still at school, whether at St Austell or elsewhere. Regular annual awards were made, usually £15 per year, and in 1961, two girls received £24 each for the year at £8 per term.

Means tested maintenance and clothing awards continued to be made by the LEA. Until 1957 when a new scale was introduced by the LEA, the number of awards was low, often with more being rejected because the family income was too high, than granted. At the end of the period, however, the number increased with, for instance, ten boys

ST. AUSTELL GRAMMAR SCHOOL FOR GIRLS
UNIFORM

Junior and Middle School

Girls wear a green pinafore frock of the regulation school pattern with a belt of the same material.

From the Fifth Form upwards a green skirt may be worn.

White blouses.

Green knickers.

Green gaberdine mackintosh.

Green woollen cardigan.

Green V necked pullover without sleeves.

Beret.

Shoe bag.

Indoor shoes.

Purse on a strap or string.

Blazer. (Not necessary until the 3rd term)

Socks (Green), or full length fawn or beige lisle or stretch nylon stockings. In the summer WHITE short socks may be worn. One pair of socks must always be left in school for changing in wet weather.

N.B. FORMS I and II must wear fawn knee length socks or long stockings in wool or stretch nylon during the Winter and Spring terms.
(Parents may knit these.)

PHYSICAL EDUCATION UNIFORM

Green shorts for P.E. lessons. (Pattern: Butterick 523. Procurable at the Singer Sewing Machine: Market House, St. Austell.)

A white P.E. blouse. (This may be ordered from the school during the first week.)

White or black gym shoes.

A THICK dark green Pullover with sleeves. (Pattern: Weldons Knitwear. A 1213. Price 4d. Double knitting wool. Procurable at A. POPE, Fore Street, St. Austell.) This is for P.E. only and may not be worn in school, except in extremely cold weather when special permission will be given.

Girls' School Uniform List 1950s. These detailed requirements were issued to the parents of each new pupil

and fifteen girls being successful in their claims for maintenance, clothing allowances having, apparently, ceased as a separate award.

With the end of clothes rationing, uniform regulations became clearer and were more strictly enforced. While the girls continued to wear green, in 1958 the boys abandoned their purple for black blazers, a black tie with diagonal red and gold stripes and a new badge. Head gear appears to have been the greatest bone of contention. Adrian Thomas (1960-66) remembers clearly that boys had to 'wear their caps at all times whilst outside school and in uniform. Caps had to be raised to any teachers whom you met in the street'. There was a similar rule for girls with their berets and later their hats. The green beret 'had to be worn at all times with winter uniform – even when travelling on the bus to and from school' Sylvia Ronaldson (Hooper 1953-8) remembers. Staff

were expected to patrol the park to see that all obeyed! Penny Trethewey (1958-64) confessed to me, after nearly 50 years, 'Do you realise that after you drove through Roche each morning, the girls at the bus stop took off their hats – a small act of rebellion, I suppose.' Unless exceptionally tall, young boys had to wear short trousers for the first three years, and ties were an essential part of a schoolboy's attire. It was a strict rule that girls had a pair of indoor shoes which had to be worn when in the building, a wire pigeon hole being provided under each coat rack. Many were the excuses for not wearing them, including this one, quoted in the 1961 Magazine: 'I'm not wearing my indoor shoes: they're in my form room. I took them up to show I had them in school'! Another source of complaint was the 'green bags, knickers with long legs, granny knickers' Doris Lobb (1951-1959) which were worn during the first two or three years, and for gym.

Stars and stripes continued to be the marks of reward and punishment, and great was the trepidation at the possibility of gaining a stripe. Caroline Nash (Rowe 1957-64) used to 'save up my stripes and present them to my parents on my birthday, hoping they wouldn't be too cross!' Corporal punishment was used only rarely, in the Boys' School, although there were the odd 'blows' in the classroom from board rubbers and rubber tubing. Apparently, it was Mr 'Dickie' Richardson's boast that he never missed a boy within 12 paces with a piece of chalk! The fear of punishment was often as potent as the real thing. My researcher remembers being in the 1st year and, with a friend, ignoring the rule forbidding foraging in the shrubbery for lost tennis balls. 'Once in there, we forgot the balls and pretended to be exploring the Amazon. Some time later we crawled out, covered in greenfly, to find ourselves at the feet of two mistresses on duty. They looked very serious but moved on, and we spent the rest of the day, fearful, expecting to be summoned to the HM's study. Nothing happened'.

School trips abroad began to develop as a feature of the school year. The first venture by the Boys' was in 1951 when three VIth Form boys went to France and this was followed, the next year, by a party of 32 who went on a tour of France and Belgium at Easter with Mr Johns. In 1957 and 1958 there were visits to Paris led by Mr

Lincoln, enjoyed by 61 boys in total. A few girls also enjoyed visits to France, such as to Normandy in 1955 with Miss Castle, or to Heidelberg and the Rhine in Germany in 1957, to improve their language skills, and in 1952, Miss Husband and her sister took seventeen girls on the first of three annual trips to Switzerland during the summer holidays, to walk in the mountains and enjoy the spectacular scenery. These were joint trips with Bude Grammar School where Miss Joan Husband was teaching. Beryl Vivian, who had been a pupil from 1942-9 and was by then teaching, remembers accompanying the party as 'an additional help'. In 1960, four young members of staff, Misses Alford, Bowly, Stone and I took some 30 girls for a holiday to the Italian Dolomites and Venice. In the same year Marlene Behennah went to Denmark under the auspices of UNESCO. Thus began a tradition of encouraging St Austell's young people to spread their wings beyond the UK.

Expeditions continued in this country too; for example, Dr Wilson's Science VIth Form girls going to London and Exeter for conferences, Dr Matthews taking three biologists to the Isles of Scilly for a Marine Biology course and my taking a small party of historians to London – Penny Trethewey remembers buying a sheet of wrapping paper in Harrods 'just so I could walk around carrying a Harrods bag'. From 1958 Mr Farnham-Flower took small groups of boys Youth Hostelling to Dartmoor, Shropshire and Scotland. The Upper VI Science boys went to a lecture in Plymouth in 1956, entitled 'Why we believe in atoms and what we can do with them'. Miss Husband and Mrs Richardson continued to take large parties to Folk Dance Festivals in Cornwall and, in May 1951 there was a School expedition to Paignton Zoo and the River Dart, remembered by Glenda Bullock (Bath 1949-54), possibly combined with the Boys' who made a similar trip. In 1952, nine boys went to London to take part in the Cornish presentation of an episode in *The Wesley Tapestry* at the Methodist Association of Youth Clubs' Annual Rally in the Royal Festival Hall – a memorable part of the trip, apparently, being sleeping in the war time underground shelters. There were also visits to notable dramatic productions in the county such as *The Taming of the Shrew* in Truro Cathedral in 1951, and *King Lear* at the Minack Theatre in 1960 – there was

no resident, professional theatre in Cornwall or Plymouth and these visits were important. Brian Strathen (1949-54) remembers being very excited as a member of a party from the Boys' School going to London after the Coronation in 1953 – few had been beyond Plymouth before. Miss Harry took 29 girls to a Royal Academy Exhibition in Truro in 1952, and, in the same year, nineteen girls saw an Exhibition at the County Record Office in Truro with Miss Husband. Prestigious national orchestras made annual visits to Cornwall and St Austell young people were given the opportunity to hear them. In 1953, 75 boys heard the Royal Philharmonic in Truro Cathedral, and the following year a party of girls went to Truro to hear Sir John Barbirolli and the Hallé Orchestra. The boys enjoyed many expeditions to sporting events such as 30 boys going to the AAA championships at White City in 1953, combining it with ballet at the Royal Festival Hall and Sonja Henje's Ice Show. 56 attended a Schoolboy International, England v Eire, at Plymouth in 1957 and another party went to London for an Athletics competition, the Commonwealth v USA. Such visits were not confined to the VIth Form – in 1951, Miss Husband began taking whole years of juniors to Restormel Castle. That year it was Forms II, and the following year, Forms I and II. In 1954, IVB of the Boys' School visited the Gas Works, and in 1960 there was an electronics excursion to the Telephone Exchange.

Visiting speakers were still an important addition to the curriculum. Miss Camous was instrumental in persuading many cultural bodies to come to St Austell, usually promoting languages, to which the boys were invited. For instance, in 1954 it was the French Players and *Le Bourgeois Gentilhomme*, and in 1958 Anthony Hopkins' *Intimate Opera*. There was also joint attendance for regular musical presentations – a piano recital in 1952 and a Leon Goosens concert in 1955, for example. According to Alan Hutt, the piano in the Hall was a superb Bechstein grand, belonging to St Austell Music Society, and this was a further encouragement for concerts. This was the period of Harold Macmillan's 'Wind of Change' and there were many speakers from commonwealth countries, who addressed the boys not only on African issues but also on areas as disparate as Fiji, British Guiana and Jamaica. Walter Julian, an Old Boy

Above: *Football XI early 1950s with Mr Brinkworth and Mr Ken Hunter (courtesy K Hunter)*
Below and oposite page: *Staff v VIth Form Hockey match, March 1961. As usual it was 'won' by the VIth Form, but a good time was had by all*

and the son of Mr Julian, talked about working as a mining engineer in Peru, and Laurence Martin, son of Mr Martin, who was pursuing an academic career in the USA as well as in Britain, talked of his experiences in America. The VIth Form boys were given a lecture on *National Service in the Army* in 1950 – a time when virtually all eighteen year old boys had to do two years military service. In 1951, Freddie Grisewood talked to the girls on *Aspects of the BBC*, and in 1959, Sir John Hunt addressed the boys on the recently established Duke of Edinburgh Award. A particularly topical lecture and lantern slide was given to both Schools in 1953 by Eric Shipton, after the first ascent of Everest, as were films and commentaries on the Coronation. This is just a small sample of the wide ranging issues covered.

The importance of extra curricular activities in the life of both Schools did not diminish. Sporting activities became more diverse with a gymnastics club and the introduction of basket ball by Mr Jones, in 1952, with the hard tennis court being resurfaced with appropriate new

markings. The 'usual' team games of football and cricket were supplemented by a greater emphasis on athletics following the appointment of Mr Ken Hunter in 1952 and a mini athletics arena being created by Mr Body and the boys in 1958. Each year boys usually won events in Cornwall Schools AAA meetings and many went on to represent Cornwall in the All England Championships. The annual competition with Sutton High School thus assumed an even greater focus. Football was played competitively, not only by a 1st XI but increasingly by Under 16, 15 and 14 XIs, with the most successful year being 1961/2 when 105 matches were played, 68 of which were won and six drawn and the Under 15 team won the County Shield. Regularly boys played in representative matches, East Cornwall Schools, Cornwall Youth XI and Cornwall Schools XI. Cricket usually managed eight to ten matches, with mixed fortunes. Tennis was in its infancy in 1950 but gradually developed, in spite of lack of opposition – in 1954 there were four matches, two of which were rained off – until House matches were played in 1960. Rugby still

Trampolining hits the Quad in the Girls' School 1962

did not feature significantly in Mid Cornwall at this time.

The girls continued to make a modest impact on the sporting activities in the County. They, too, were inspired to indulge in athletics by the opening of the Par running track in 1957, which coincided with the South West Athletics Championships. Diana Shaw and Patricia Pomeroy were selected for the All-England Championships at Southampton. Each School continued its internal Sports Days. There was competition in a wide range of events with points being won to contribute to House totals. Of course, there were also inter House Matches in all team games, often ferociously contested. Hockey was pursued by the girls with enthusiasm in spite of the difficulties of those who lived far beyond walking distance from St Austell. Brenda Taylor (May 1955-61), a dedicated goal-keeper, remembers how trying it was if hockey practice finished a little late and she and friends arrived, with all their kit, at the bus station, to see the St Dennis bus disappearing. There would fol-low a dash through the town to catch the bus at the Truro Road traffic lights. They never did! The team enjoyed some success but never approached the heights of the 1920s. One memorable moment for them came in 1953 when, for the first time, they beat the boys, 4-2, in the annual hockey match! The netball team won the inter Grammar School Tournament in 1954, for the first time since 1940 and the final, crowning glory of the Girls' School came in 1962 when they won, for the first time, the Watkins Cup competed for amongst the girls of the County. Heather Stout (Best 1955-62) was a member of the team along with Sylvia Thornley, Susan Burton and Jill Truscott, and remembers that 'we felt, very strongly, from the opposing team and the umpire, that we were not supposed to win it – the other team played 'proper tennis' and we were self taught.'

Music continued to be a really important part of many pupils' school experience. The choirs of each School performed separately providing a very positive public face on occasions such as Carol Services, Rededication Services, Concerts and Speech Days, as well as enjoying special events,

Girls' School Choir and Orchestra with Mr Bending performing in the Hall in March 1959. In the background is the memorial lectern made by Mr T Crabb and now in use in St Austell College

most notably the Girls' Senior Choir appearing on the BBC's *Let the People Sing* series in 1962. By this time they were being conducted by Mr Bending, their first full time male member of staff. On one memorable occasion the choirs united to give a joint performance of *St John's Passion* in the Parish Church in 1951. This is particularly well remembered by Raymond Trudgian (1948-55) who met his future wife, Angela Mitchell (1947-54), during rehearsals. Mr Mallaband was the moving force here, having a foot in both camps as music master for both Schools, and there were two further joint productions of Passion music before he left in 1956. Thereafter Mr Hutt was the music master in the Boys' School and Miss Hoskin and then Mr Bending in the Girls'.

The Girls' School developed an orchestra during the 1950s which performed in a concert for the first time in 1958. Carol Eveleigh (Tremaine 1955-62) began playing the violin as a junior and remembers the thrill of being promoted from 3rd to 2nd violin! Although the orchestra was not well balanced, being very thin in woodwind, she

enjoyed making music communally. In 1961 the Senior and Junior Choirs joined the orchestra in a concert with Gwendoline Mason and her harp. Later in 1961, a Middle School Choir, too, was formed in the Girls' School. The Boys' School, too, developed an orchestra, particularly after the introduction of string and woodwind lessons, and this performed in public for the first time, in July 1960. The late '50s saw a flowering of music in the Boys' School with the beginning of an annual House Music Competition in 1958 and the formation of a Jazz Group. Both Senior Choirs, and later the orchestras, contributed to County and local Music Festivals, continuing to win honours.

Early dramatic performances in the Boys' School were largely form plays produced during the course of a year. In 1953, however, the Boys' presented, to celebrate the Coronation, an historical pageant, *Royalty through the Ages*, with all the costumes made by the boys. It began as an idea thrown by Mr Martin to Lower VI Arts to produce years I–IV in some sketches and 'it just growed'! In 1952/3, there were nine form plays

ST. AUSTELL GRAMMAR SCHOOL FOR GIRLS

presents Scenes from

" *A Midsummer Night's Dream* "

by William Shakespeare

SPEECH DAY, JULY 21ST, 1960

Peter Quince and his friends rehearse, and eventually present, a play before Duke Theseus and his bride in Athens.

Quince	Veronica Steward	Puck	Marlene Snell
Snug (Lion)	Mary Kirkham	Titania	Valerie Arthur
Bottom (Pyramus)	Brenda Davies	Peaseblossom	Rosemary Price
Flute (Thisbe)	Sheila Trickey	Cobweb	Trudy Endean
Snout (Wall)	Jean Wearing	Moth	Patricia Bradfield
Starveling (Moonshine)	Dorcas Beer	Mustardseed	Linda Evans

Theseus	Dawn Wilkinson
Hippolyta	Sally Winstanley
Philostrate	Victoria Stirling
Demetrius	Carol Bebb
Helena	Jane Mills
Lysander	Maryse Gordon
Hermia	Carole Truscott

The recorders are played by Frances Tresize and Patricia Bradfield.

Programme of Girls' School play presented at Speech Day 1960

but by 1958 there were only two. This was because the arrival of Mr FF Farnham-Flower, in 1957, saw more lavish and public annual performances. In 1961 the new House Speech Competition also saw the focus move away from form activities. The Girls' performed mostly on Speech Days, such as *A Midsummer Night's Dream* in 1960, while the Boys' gave evening performances on three consecutive days, such as *Noah* by Andre Obey, December 11/12/13th 1958, *Macbeth* in 1960 and Gogol's *The Government Inspector* in 1960/1. Dorothy Sayers' *The Devil to Pay* was reviewed very favourably in the Times Education Supplement in 1961/2. A contemporary value judgement comes from Caroline Nash (Rowe 1957-64) who remembers 'great Boys' School plays, with John Nettles and Richard Turner taking the leads' – she was in a privileged position as her father was Mr JHR Rowe, the Boys' School Latin master! The boys were also entertained throughout this period by the much anticipated and uncensored VIth Form Revue which continued in spite of some 'carpeting' of those whose imagination caused offence.

Societies covering a range of other interests continued to flourish. The Boys' School Debating Society tackled such subjects as: 'That the Festival of Britain is a waste of time and money' in 1951,

Above & opposite page: *Boys' School production of The Government Inspector 1961 including John Nettles, David Townsend, Ian Pawlby, Richard Turner and Clive Mitchell (courtesy Alan Townsend)*

which lost, and, in 1957, during the Suez Crisis: 'That this house deplores the recent British and French action in Egypt', which was also defeated. The Girls' Debating Society for years IV, V and VI, covered a similar range of subjects. In 1959/60, the Boys' saw the formation of a Philosophical Society which provided a mixed programme of debates, play readings, discussions and music, while the Scientific Society enjoyed ten lectures and fifteen films, drawing much from internal expertise. A mock election was held, with the Girls' School in 1950, but history does not record the winner. A Film and Photographic Society was formed by Mr Gates in 1952 and remodelled as the Film Society in 1955, while, in 1960, Miss Davies formed a Writers Club. A Chess Club made a modest start, also in the Girls' School in 1959. An annual Art Exhibition was held on Speech Day in the Boys' School and in 1955 this was expanded to include Woodwork. In 1958 an annual Bird and Tree Competition, in conjunction with the RSPB, made its appearance in the Boys' School for the first time.

The Tuesday Dancing Class continued to be embraced enthusiastically and by 1962, Mr Wearing and Mr Lincoln had joined Miss Bridgewater in running it for years IV, V and VI. End of term parties were enjoyed by all. An unnamed male contemporary felt that it was 'turning them gradually from baby elephants to young gazelles'! The Scout Group and the Girl Guide Company, too, continued to prosper. The Scouts celebrated their 21st birthday in 1958 with a party and the issue of a handbook. They had won the Crowder Trophy, a Senior Scout County Competition, the previous year, and JM Goss had become the company's first Queen's Scout – they had good reason to rejoice. By 1962, there were four further Queen's Scouts. The Guides held their weekly meetings on Friday after school, and Carol Eveleigh (Tremaine 1955-62) remembers that it was a pleasant change to be able to wear her Guide uniform rather than her school uniform! They were enthusiastic in their pursuit of skills to achieve badges, but also enjoyed the annual 'outings'. Miss Husband continued to be the Captain and I helped after my appointment, contributing to burnt sausages on a company hike around the Gribben.

The Duke of Edinburgh Award Scheme began in the Boys' School in 1958 with 26 boys tak-

John Goss of 2nd St Austell Scout Troop receiving his Queen's Scout badge from Mr Brinkworth 1957

ing part and by 1959, eight had completed the bronze award. The first gold award was achieved in 1960/1, together with two silver and a further five bronze.

The House system, the same three Houses in both Schools – Tewington, Trenance and Treverbyn, still provided a focus for corporate activity. Scores were compiled from numerous activities from sporting, through Music and Speech competitions to the plus and minus func-

tions of stars and stripes. Membership of a House was important, and, when assigned to one in the Ist Form, a pupil stayed there throughout her/his school career.

Speech Day was a huge event during the school year, especially in the Girls' School. The whole morning was given over to preparing for this day when the School was on show. Doris Lobb remembers: 'prize winners were scrutinized to make sure they were clean, tidy and in absolutely

Above: *Lady Baden-Powell visited the Girls' School in 1961 for a County Jamboree. We think that these are not actually our guides, but visiting ones. Definitely our building.*

Below: *Boys' School Speech Day in the Hall 1960 (courtesy Alan Townsend)*

Girls' School Upper VI just before amalgamation, in July 1962. **Back Row:** *Ruth Tregunna, Angela Tully, Frances King, Gillian Treseder, Sylvia Thornley, Heather Best, Susan Burton, Jacqueline Evison.* **Middle Row:** *Barbara Grose, Hilary Roberts, Penny Winstanley, Jacky Reeves, Ingrid Jones, Jill Truscott, Elinor Griffiths, Vicky Stirling, Carol Tremaine, Avril Williams.* **Front Row:** *Nancy Dingle, Marie Bennetto, Cathryn Manning, Mary Locke, Miss Husband, Miss Camous, Pauline Clark (Head Girl), Elizabeth Clyma, Mary Giles, Anne Behenna, Jennifer Palmer*

correct school uniform, and that they knew how to take their book or certificate and shake hands at the same time.' The Choir would rehearse until perfection was achieved and chairs and furniture would be moved appropriately. During the afternoon those who had not won a prize heard the proceedings in their form rooms which had been wired up for a sound system. After the formal proceedings dancing, gymnastics or a play was performed. Elizabeth Burroughs (Clyma 1955-63) remembers that *Everyman* was put on in 1958 in the Quad. 'God was played by Kay Rosevear, complete with long white gown and long white beard. It was decided that she should declaim her lines from the roof of the covered way. This entailed

her scrambling out of one of the windows of the chemistry lab, and then clambering back in again. This was quite a feat for Kay who was not the tallest member of the form, even when not encumbered by her costume!' The staff were expected to wear their full academic dress and Hilary Bilkey (Aggett 1950-57) was particularly impressed by Dr Wilson's 'lovely red one'. In the Boys' School the proceedings always included a rendering of *Gaudeamus Igitur* performed, Alan Hutt suspects, with more gusto than understanding. In 1960/1 the Boys' School introduced two Speech Days – Juniors, years I, II and III, and Seniors IV, V, and VI.

National events, too, impinged on daily life.

Austell Bay returning from a royal tour. Summer Term, 1960, began a day late because of the birth of Prince Andrew and the wedding of Princess Margaret – even left wing political thought in the Boys' School was able to join in!

The health of all school children was becoming an increasing concern for Local Education Authorities. In the summer term, 1954, the School Medical Service launched a new initiative to combat tuberculosis. A mass radiography unit gave chest x-rays to all members of the middle and senior school, with some selective Mantoux skin tests to determine natural resistance to TB. Negative reactions resulted in BCG vaccinations. During the '50s, nationally, there were worrying outbreaks of polio (poliomyelitis) which did spread alarm. In 1958 all the pupils were vaccinated against the disease.

In 1953 the Secretary for Education, in Cornwall, expressed his concern at the loss of schooling at elections when schools always seemed to be used as polling stations, causing the whole school to be shut for the day. A circular asked governing bodies if they had a suitable, discrete room with an outside door. The Lower Old Kitchen was suggested and was used appropriately.

A mini scandal was aired in the local and national press when, in 1961, the Duke of Edinburgh landed on the top field, in his helicopter, to speak with those who were working towards his Award. For some reason Miss Camous had refused to allow the girls to attend and afterwards, the Duke is reputed to have asked: 'Where are the girls?' She had to admit to having made a tactical error and apologised to the Secretary for Education.

There were, sadly, deaths of long serving members of staff. Miss Lewis died in 1951, having only a short period of retirement, and Mr Holland in 1952, while still working, after fifteen years of service. Then, in 1959, Miss Bond, too, died having enjoyed only nine years of retirement during which she contributed much to the community with her voluntary work as well as using her experience and wisdom as a member of various committees. She had stayed in St Austell and her funeral at the Parish Church was attended by many staff and pupils from both Schools as well as a large congregation from the general public. She was a much loved lady.

Early in 1962 Miss Camous announced that

In February 1952, Allan Barrett (1946-53) and his friends noticed that the Brewery flag had been lowered to half-mast. 'The caretaker told us "George is dead" and we thought he meant George Brinkworth, but he meant the king, George VI'. Roger Parnell (1950-55) recalls how they were all called to a special assembly in the Hall, mid morning, to be told the news. A service was held on the day of the funeral, February 15th, including a two minutes silence. The Coronation of the Queen, in June 1953, was celebrated with a day's holiday, nationally, and both Schools saw *A Queen is Crowned* at the Odeon. In those days when very few families had television, films at the cinema were an important medium for giving visual accounts of significant events, such as *The Ascent of Everest* at the Capitol in January 1954, as well as cultural productions, such as *Romeo and Juliet, Hamlet, Henry V, Wuthering Heights* and so on at the Odeon. In April 1954, some boys were up early to see the Royal Yacht Britannia in St

she would be retiring in the summer. There followed huge discussions, both locally and at County level about the future of the Schools. Eventually it was decided that merger would take place, and that St Austell would revert to one Grammar School. It was to be a gradual merger with the new Ist Forms and the VIth being the only ones to be taught together, initially. Letters drafted by JG Harries, Secretary for Education and signed by the Chair of the Governors, were sent to all parents. Mr Brinkworth, automatically, became the Headmaster but the post of Deputy, which was to be a woman, was to be applied for. There were five applicants, four of whom came from out of the county, and Miss Husband was appointed. There was much consternation among the Girls' School staff about the merger, and, eventually, eleven resigned, it has to be said, with prompting from Miss Camous. This, together with some 'natural wastage' from the Boys' School, actually eased the situation as there was little controversy over the appointment of Heads of Department. Mr Martin became the Senior Master, following the retirement of Mr Richardson after 39 years of teaching Geography to several generations of boys and girls. Miss Daniel resigned as Secretary, leaving Miss Davey as Headmaster's Secretary and the two laboratory assistants were obviously still needed.

There was not universal joy among the pupils at the prospect of a large mixed school and Richard Turner (1956-63), as editor of the Boys' Magazine, wrote that life is full of challenges but 'when the upheaval is so momentous as to upset the whole equilibrium of school life, there are bound to be grave misgivings. Juniors are excited but this will be mollified when they discover that to be beaten at maths by a girl is the most humiliating experience yet suffered by man.' Many of the girls had similar sentiments. Penny Trethewey (1958-64) remembers 'we were all horrified when the school went co-educational' but Janet Mugridge (Goudge 1956-63) reacted 'with glee. Delighted. As an only child and so without brothers, this made me more confident with boys and this helped when I went to University.'

As a very young member of staff, I received an excellent start to my teaching career in the Girls' School. Miss Camous was strict disciplinarian, and everyone in the School, especially me, knew exactly what was expected of them. There was never any possibility that we were there just to teach, there was always extra to do. I was quite sure that, like Mary Tudor and Calais, I would have 'chairs' carved on my heart! I have always been grateful for my introduction to my career. However, there are many who do not have such rosy memories. In her anxiety to encourage Cornish schoolgirls to behave according to her standards in order to make the most of their opportunities, Miss Camous could, and did, cause resentment. Her referring to the 'complacent Cornish' and 'Cornish cabbages' did not go down well, nor did 'Cornish clod hoppers' when there was a mini rebellion against the introduction of Greek Dancing. She often inspired fear. Vicky Crossingham (Bethel 1954-60) says: 'I was terrified walking past Miss Camous' room as often the door would open and she would call me in for a chat on my progress.' For Elizabeth West (Moon 1959-65) 'she seemed to know all the pupils by name' and 'between periods would stand outside her office and greet pupils as they moved to their next class'. She taught French with enthusiasm and could never be accused of being a head who lived in an ivory tower. The end of her reign was certainly the end of an era.

8. THE FINAL FLOURISHING 1962 – 75

When the new mixed Grammar School opened its doors in September, 1962, it was very different from the first one in 1908. Pupil numbers had risen from 101 to 785 and were to continue to rise until reaching a peak of 903 just before reorganisation of secondary education in St Austell in 1971. There were now 43 full time members of the teaching staff and seven part time, compared with the seven full time in 1908. The buildings had expanded enormously with facilities which could not have been dreamed of 54 years before. In 1962, very few of the nearly 900 people who began that term could have foreseen that the School as it was had less than ten years to run.

The new regime was Mr Brinkworth as Headmaster, with his office in the old Boys' building, Miss Husband as Deputy Head, with her office in the old Girls' building, and Mr Martin as Senior Master. Fourteen new teachers had been appointed, representing most departments. Miss Daniel's resignation as the Girls' School Secretary resulted in the need for an extra fourteen hours per week to be filled. In spite of the LEA's initial promise that no member of the support staff would lose their job, in fact the caretaking/cleaning staff was reduced to one Head Caretaker, one groundsman/stoker, one full time cleaner and 66 part time cleaning hours. This meant there was to be one fewer groundsman and one fewer full-time caretaker although there were to be eight more cleaning hours per week.

There was much to be done to create one school from the previous two. Sheer size itself could have been a major problem and Mr Brinkworth's plan was to divide the school, horizontally, into three – Junior, Middle and Senior. Six tutors, a woman and a man for each section, were appointed to be responsible for discipline, reporting and general well being, while remaining as teachers in their own subject areas. Messrs Wolstenholme, Lincoln and Wearing, and Misses Bridgewater, Tyzzer and I were appointed with appropriate remuneration. Curriculum matters were to remain the province of Heads of Department whose allowances largely were raised. There were more graded posts available. Of course there was not immediate harmony

Prefects and House Captains 1962-3. **Back Row:** *J Williams, G Knox, J Church, J James, G Jeffrey, I Pawlby, D Whitworth, A Job, N Laycock, J Atkinson, D Goldsworthy, D Yelland.* **Middle Row:** *Patricia Bennetto, Catherine Parnell, Carole Borlase, Frances King, Barbara Grose, Dawn Wilkinson, Janet Goudge, Linda Willis, Christine Bailey, Frances Truscott, Diane Pascoe, Kathryn Treleaven, Susan Thomas, Alice James, Gail Nicholls, Margaret Crocker, Carol Davies, Gillian Mugford, Linda Barrett.* **Front Row:** *R Nile, D Townsend, G Yelland, R Bullen, R Turner (Head Boy), Mr Martin, Mr Brinkworth, Miss Husband, Elizabeth Clyma (Head Girl), Sylvia Thornley, Jennifer Palmer, Kathryn Fugler, Wendy Ingham*

The Language Laboratory 1966

amongst the staff, and, until 1967 there were separate staff rooms which did not encourage social integration, but generally departments worked well together for the common good.

The pupils, too, were not totally integrated initially. The VIth formers were; it would have been uneconomic as well as undesirable to teach them separately. The new Ist Forms continued their mixed education as they had enjoyed it in their primary schools. For the rest it was a gradual process, achieved only in September 1966. There was a mixed reaction to the amalgamation, inevitably, but Sue Palmer (1962-7) says ' I was part of the first intake for the mixed school and, having also experienced an all-girls school for my last two years at Orpington, can say I definitely preferred the mixed school life!' Of course there was now a mixed body of prefects with an appointed Head Boy and Girl. The first were Richard Turner and Elizabeth Burroughs (Clyma). I suspect that the VIth formers integrated much more quickly and happily than the staff!

Physically there was much to be done to convert the buildings to mixed use. Cloakrooms had to be adapted and, in particular the outside boys'

urinals were a disgrace. Provision of staff toilets, too, left much to be desired and the Governors repeatedly requested the LEA to provide adequate facilities. The situation was not resolved until 1967 when £5,000 was granted for a new staff room, built between the old Boys' School building and the Hall, with appropriate cloakrooms. There was also a need for sufficient hard surface play ground areas, but this, too, was frequently shelved by the LEA because of lack of resources for 'minor works'. There was better news on the curriculum front. In June 1966 ECLP, the major local clay company, gave £2,000 to establish a language laboratory for joint use by their senior staff training, by students from St Austell Technical Institute and by the School. Comments from pupils in the School Magazine include one from a Vth Form wag – 'On two afternoons a week employees of a certain company … come to learn how to sell their products to the continent. You can imagine a Frenchman being introduced to a salesman "Ici l'argile (clay)" or perhaps it ought to be "Ici LP"!' Julie Prophet (Edwards 1962-9) admits to being 'terrified of it when it was first introduced'.

By the end of that year the LEA granted £6,250

It was not all hard work! Upper VI boys demonstrate their skills with the Triceratops they constructed in the summer of 1963. Those involved included Adrian Job, David Townsend, Richard Turner and Mike Hands

for two Art Rooms to be erected on the grass tennis courts next to the Brewery. This removed the necessity of the long trek to Carclaze Infants' School. However, public examinations could no longer be accommodated within the School and the Church Hall was hired which presented logistical problems of getting desks there and set up, as well as VIth Form 'runners' being available in the event of a 'crisis'. By 1967 the School was considered to be overcrowded with 788 and rising and, bearing in mind the arrival of the VIth Form from Fowey Grammar School in September 1967, the LEA granted £19,850 for the provision of a Sixth Form Centre to be ready by 1969. The playing fields also could not accommodate changing needs and in 1970 work began on an all weather pitch. Progress was painfully slow because of difficulties of access from Hillside Road, as well as contractual problems, and it was not finally complete by 1973, although parts were in use by 1971. In the meantime the UDC football ground at Poltair continued to be used as a 'temporary measure'. There was also, of course, much tweaking to bring the premises up to date. For instance, in 1963

there was a Governors' request for each room to have a power point; most did not. Much was not tackled at all. For instance there was still no room for sick pupils before 1973. That was left for the new comprehensive.

However the School flourished and certainly incorporated the best of the old Boys' and Girls' Schools as well as developing its own practices and ethos. The curriculum expanded to meet developing needs with the core remaining as it was. More pupils were taking the extra 'Scholarship' paper at Advanced Level, and there was more choice available. For instance, Mathematics at A Level was taken as three separate subjects – Pure, Pure and Applied and Further. In 1969 Economics was introduced in the VIth Form – O Level at the end of the Lower VI and A Level at the end of the Upper. Three years later British Constitution, later to become Political Studies, was introduced on a similar programme, with Geology and Spanish also available at O Level. This meant that by 1972 nineteen subjects were taken at A Level and 27 at O Level. In addition to these, in 1969 CSE, Certificate of Secondary

Upper VI Arts 1965-6. Five years later they would not have been wearing school uniform!

Education, was introduced nationally. This was aimed largely at the less academic pupil, subjects with a Grade 1 being accepted as the equivalent of an O Level pass. This was useful as a 'safety net' particularly for Mathematics, the Sciences and Languages with the gradual introduction of the necessity for qualification in some subjects for specific careers. It also enabled 'new' subjects to be introduced, such as PE in 1973.

Success in public examinations continued its upward trend. In 1962, 49 pupils took subjects at A Level with 95 passes, while in 1973, 101 achieved a total of 151 passes, 57 achieving at least three passes and a further 22 at least one. At O Level, in 1962, 116 pupils achieved a total of 453 passes and in the summer of 1973, 142 achieved 663 passes, and a further 63, mostly Lower VI, 65 passes. There was also an examination at Christmas, partly for re-takes but also for the Vth Form taking subjects early, particularly Mathematics, Foreign History and German. In 1973, a further 112 passes were achieved.

Destinations of school leavers at sixteen, after

O Level, did not change significantly with there still being much employment available locally, in both local and national establishments, as well as professional training schemes, such as in law, obviating the necessity of reading for a university degree. Post A Level leavers also progressed to very similar destinations to those of the 1950s, when the break-through had really come and a wider range of courses and careers had become available. In 1963 seventeen boys and eight girls embarked on university courses from Electrical Engineering to Theology and English Literature to History in all parts of the country from Durham to Cambridge and Leeds to London as well as at the relatively new Colleges of Advanced Technology. By 1974 this had increased to seventeen girls and a comparable number of boys following similarly diverse courses. There was a steady stream of both boys and girls gaining entrance to Oxbridge colleges, with 1973 being a particularly vintage year when seven gained admission, Michael Abbott, Charles Blacker, Helen Duckworth, Judith Gunn, Robin Marshall, Robert Merriman and Stephen

Above: *Football 1st XI 1970-1.* **Back Row:** *Mr Ken Hunter, D Bishop (Res.), E Giles, S Lethbridge, R Snowden (Capt.), M Best, P Trevivian, R Merriman, E Wickett (Res.)* **Front Row:** *R Hurrell, J Gill, R Marshall, R Nicholls, P Cornelius* **Below:** *Football Celebration Dinner 1966-7 (Courtesy K Hunter)*

Parry-Jones to read for degrees ranging from Mathematics to Archaeology and Anthropology.

Increasing numbers, particularly of girls, were embarking on teacher training and nursing, and accountancy was becoming popular. One boy embarked on an HND (Higher National Diploma) in Hotel Keeping and Catering at Torquay, part of the South Devon Technical College – at that time considered to be the best in the country – and two girls began HNDs in Business Studies at Ealing Technical College in London. Apprenticeships were still available and many boys began their careers in engineering by this route, as did deck officers in the Merchant Navy. With the end of National Service in the late 1950s far fewer boys opted for a career in the Services although some girls broke the mould with approximately one girl per year joining one branch or another; Elizabeth Mannell gained officer entry to the WRAC in 1974. Both boys and girls entered the police force either as cadets in out of county forces – there were still cadetships available for girls at that time – or, more usually,

St. Austell Grammar School Football Club

A Season To Remember

Winners of

County Youth Cup
County Youth League
St. Austell and District League
Mid - Cornwall Under 16 League
County Under 13 Shield
Mid - Cornwall Under 13 League

CELEBRATION DINNER

to be held at the

School

on

Thursday 11th July

at

7. 30 p.m.

Miss Husband

TICKET No.   TABLE No.

Hockey 1st XI 1962-3. **Back Row:** *Gillian Coombe, Jennifer Palmer, Marian Kent, Elizabeth, Clyma, Judith Parker, Trudi Franklin, Jeanette Horner* **Front Row:** *Patricia Brock, Kathryn Treleaven (Capt), Miss Jo Stamp, Sylvia Thornley , Kay Martin, Diana Key*

joining the Devon and Cornwall Constabulary. Art and Music colleges became more accessible and there was a steady stream, particularly of girls, progressing to them.

Funding arrangements for Higher Education did not change significantly and the system of grants meant that capable students were not disadvantaged on economic grounds whatever subject area they chose to follow. The Sydney Hancock Scholarship provided some small financial support for, as yet, non traditional courses, such as HND. £5 each was given to two girls in 1967, not vast sums but undoubtedly it helped a little.

There is no record of maintenance or clothing awards by this stage, as they were made directly from County Hall. However the Fifield Bequest continued to support a few girls from St Stephens and district, regularly, for instance one received £30 in 1966 and, in 1972, four girls each received £21. The Fowey Foundation Trust revised its rules in 1964, enabling pupils from St Blazey, Par and Tywardreath to apply, along with those from Fowey. However, there is no record of the sums involved.

The school uniform remained the same, causing new Ist formers to comment that 'there seemed to be hundreds of greenfly and black ants milling about' and 'my first memory is of setting foot inside a new world of green monsters', as reported in the Magazine of 1962-3. Comprehensive lists of what was required were sent to parents of new children. School caps were still necessary for VIth Form boys at all times, and I remember tackling a group of ECLP apprentices who were capless in town during the lunch hour – and having to beat a hasty retreat! These rules, especially for the VIth Form were modified until, in the early 1970s, VIth Formers wore more or less what they liked, as long as it was decent and subdued.

The mixing of the two schools did not affect sporting activity which in the main remained single sex. Throughout this period football was arguably the most successful of the sports. Four teams regularly were fielded, 1st XI, Under 15, Under 14 and Under 13, and by the late 1960s, an 'A' XI and Under 16 as well, ensuring that talent was captured early. The 1966/7 season saw the teams play 68 matches, losing only fifteen – an enviable record. Regularly the 1st XI competed in the Luke Cup as well as playing in the County Youth League. Participation in the English Schools Trophy began in 1969/70. In 1970/71 they became the first Cornish school team to reach the second round and their greatest achievement came in March 1973 when they reached the semi finals of the competition after having travelled considerable distances to defeat other schools. Each year a number of boys played in representative teams, East Cornwall and Cornwall Schoolboys' XIs and the Cornwall Youth XI which often went on tour. For instance, in 1966/7, Lloyd Rowett and Alex Machin played in Germany while John Rich captained Cornwall Schoolboys and in 1970/71 Johnny Gill and Raymond Nicholls played for both the County Youth XI and Cornwall Grammar Schools, while Peter Trevivian played for the Youth XI and Philip Cornelius and Robert Merriman for the Schools XI. Several celebration dinners were held at the end of successful seasons for the team and friends. Roger Green (1970-77) pays tribute to Ken Hunter and the part he played in developing the boys' sporting activities: 'Ken was responsible for our success because he gave up hours of his time to coach us, and he made us believe in our ability'.

Hockey for the girls was not overwhelmingly successful but annual reports always commented on the spirit in which all games were played and the enthusiasm demonstrated even if they 'played not for the sole object of scoring goals'! An Under 15 XI also played, again contributing towards continuity. A good season was 1966/7 when they played thirteen matches, losing six and coming second in their section in the annual county hockey tournament – 'for the first time in living memory'! In 1971, being fortunate in having an all weather pitch at last, they did even better by reaching the semi finals of the tournament. The seasons ended with a Staff v. Prefects match which was usually won, by foul rather than fair means by the Prefects, who made no concessions to advancing years!

While a seven-a-side rugby team had been entered for the County Schools Competition earlier, rugby was introduced, seriously, only in 1970/71 and became surprisingly popular with the lower school. The enthusiasm of the 1st XV contributed much towards a successful first season when they won three of the four games they played. The appointment of Terry Pryor, who came from Redruth and played regularly for Cornwall and for an England A team in Romania, undoubtedly provided inspiration. Roger Green (1970-77) remembers 'with pride watching Terry play for Cornwall. My teacher plays for Cornwall and England!' Cricket was still being played on a regular basis – this was before the encroachment of public examinations from the end of May. A 1st XI and an Under 15 were fielded but there were complaints that boys were not introduced to the game young enough with the consequence that there was no nursery of talent. They played between ten and thirteen matches a season with the vast majority being won or drawn. In 1965 it was thought that with Richard Hurrell and A Campbell as opening bowlers and N Caddy's spin to follow, the school was indeed fortunate. Netball frequently managed to run three or four teams and they achieved success as well as deriving much enjoyment. The Junior team had a good year, 1968/9, when they won four of their five matches and, probably much the same players enjoyed similar success two years later in the 1st VII when two of them, Tessa Parker and Michele Harris were selected to play for the County team.

The girls were able to produce an Under 15 VI as well as the 1st Tennis VI. They were reasonably successful in their friendly matches and were able to emulate their predecessors who had won the Watkins Cup, by narrowly beating Tremough Convent in the final in 1970. In 1970/71 Badminton was introduced by Mr Holden and Miss Sonia Rowe, an Old Girl, now a teacher, who taught two groups of IIIrd formers. We have no record of future developments.

Athletics continued to be embraced wholeheartedly by both boys and girls. The sport was given a major boost in 1971 when the 'all weather' area encouraged boys particularly to participate. Teams were sent to the Mid Cornwall Sports as well as the County Athletic Championships and while boys and girls won events in the County Championships the only record we have of an athlete being selected for the County team in the English Schools Championship is Tessa Parker in 1971. The annual boys' match with Sutton High School came to an end after an unfortunate

Mr Terry Pryor with his enthusiastic young rugby players early 1970s

accident to a boy from Sutton in 1962. Cross country was re-introduced, for the first time since the very early days. During the autumn term of 1970 a series of inter school competitions was held culminating in the Inter School Road Relay run around the Carlyon Bay circuit. Martin Warne, apparently against all the odds, finally ensured that the School team won.

New on the scene came the Sailing Club. It was formed during the winter of 1963/4 and there was a strong body of staff who were enthusiasts led by Mr Peter Atkinson. There was a programme of lectures combined with boat maintenance during the winter terms culminating in sailing instruction at weekends in the summer, at Porthpean. Proficient sailors from the senior school instructed the younger ones on Friday evenings and Saturday mornings until a more ambitious idea was developed. After the Fowey River trip in 1965, when three boats 'sailed' up to Golant from Readymoney Cove on a Saturday in July it was decided to follow the example of the Cornwall Schools' Sailing Association which ran a

summer camp. So, in 1966 a weekend camp at the Adventure Training Centre at St Just-in-Roseland was organised by Mr Atkinson with Mr and Mrs Eastburn. Saturday and Sunday were spent in sailing activities, with the members taking it in turn to do the catering, watched over by Mrs Eastburn. Although the weather on this occasion was not entirely kind, the strength of the wind hampering activity on the Saturday, the venture was a success and was to become a regular feature in the School calendar. In 1970 60 members were present at some stage of the weekend when the Mylor Youth Centre was used for the first time. In 1969 five members of the VIth Form set off for a three week catamaran cruise with David Eastburn and this, too, developed into an annual event, long into the Sixth Form College era.

Extra curricular activities continued to flourish. Music and Drama took pride of place. Musical activities were many and varied. John Holland, a very young and enthusiastic teacher, was appointed in 1962 and, with Alan Hutt, the traditions were more than maintained. The Senior Choir,

Folk Dance Festival at St Austell 1967 to which the girls made their contribution

now of course mixed, had an important role to play in all School events, from the Rededication Service, begun by Mr Brinkworth in 1946 and held every Spring in the Parish Church, through the Carol Service at St John's Methodist Chapel to concerts both in and out of school. In 1966, for instance, the choir gave two performances of Brahms' *Requiem* at St Johns and St Blazey Church before proceeding on an outing to Devon where they sang Haydn's *Nelson Mass* at Buckfast Abbey, accompanied by some of the orchestra. In other years they sang in local churches from St Stephens to Lostwithiel and Victoria Road Chapel to Newquay Parish Church. The Girls' Choir continued with Alan Hutt, always singing at the St Austell Music Festival, usually with high marks and great praise. The orchestra was now well established, as was a recorder group, both of which performed occasionally in Assembly as well as at more formal occasions.

A Junior Choir was also formed and its moments of glory undoubtedly came during the Carol Services each year. These were spectacular affairs with a vast cast of performers who sang and played with great vigour – it was a miracle that the roof of St John's was not blown away! There were two performances, an afternoon one for the School and an evening one for parents and friends. The latter were always packed. They were events which are most frequently quoted by old students as being especially pleasurable. Pam Whitney (Harper 1962-7) and Phil King (1959-65) are but two and Fiona Westaway (Beard 1969-76) remembers, as a small member of the 1st Form being part of a large body of singers in a packed St John's. 'The electric atmosphere and infectious enjoyment, especially when performing a lively carol was immense. After energetic conducting, John Holland would bring the carol to an abrupt end; the sudden silence followed by thunderous applause was never to be forgotten.'

Music was a joyous activity. A reflection of the fact that 'our school is alive with music' as Betty Mitchell reported in the Magazine of 1963-4, was the House Music Competition when House Captains or their minions, cajoled and threatened

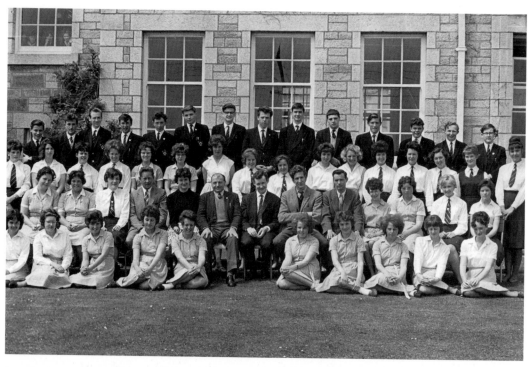

School Choir 1963 with Mr John Wearing, Miss Mary Ingram, Mr Ray Lincoln, Mr John Holland and Mr Alan Hutt

St Austell Music Festival Certificates

lesser mortals to perform. A day was given over to the event and there were opportunities for all to display their musical ability, or sometimes, lack of it! It was wide ranging and inclusive as the programme for March 1972 indicates. There were twelve classes, Junior, Senior and Open with 44 solo performers and twenty groups from choirs to ensembles. It began at 9.25 and finished about 3.45 when the external adjudicator would have pronounced and awarded the marks. There were also concerts at the end of the summer term, again reflecting the diversity of musical talent, both vocal and orchestral. It became something of a tradition that at the end, choirs, orchestra and audience should give a spirited rendering of the *The Spacious Firmament on High* which, once sung was never forgotten. One casualty was the end of term singing by the girls of *Red River Valley*. It was not officially banned, it just died away in the new environment. The media did not ignore the School either. In 1963 the Girls' Choir performed on Westward TV, as it was then called, and in 1965, 62 members of the Senior Choir descended on Westward's studios to record Haydn's *Te Deum*, amongst other pieces, to be broadcast on the religious programme *Reflection*.

The activities of 1970-71 were recounted, anonymously, in the Magazine thus, with apologies to Longfellow:

As the weeks and months have flown by
We musicians have been busy,
Have been actively engaged in
Making music without voices,
With our flutes, drums, horns and oboes.
In the month of dull October
Folk from Truro to Okehampton
Were enchanted by the voices,
Voices raised in heavenly chanting
To the heights of the Cathedral.
Followed early in December
By a visit to the Church Hall
With my fellow instrumentalists
Under our handsome conductor
And our famed and revered leader,
There we rendered with distinction
Rendered some well-loved Beethoven
To Carlyn's great satisfaction
To the adjudicator's horror!

All too soon our croaking voices
Struggled with the tricky verses
Of a certain foreign carol,
Of the JVH arrangements
And the well known Christmas carols.
Not content with two nights singing
And an afternoon in St Johns
The ever eager Junior Choir
Had their Gospel Songs recorded,
Had them broadcast on the radio,
Broadcast on Midday Parade.
All the pupils and their parents
Have enjoyed the 'Silver Trumpet'
Have enjoyed the Juniors' singing.
So Spring arrived and brought a change
Brought us musicians to the rooms
Of the New Block next the Brewery.
Our Senior Choirs bravely challenged,
Choirs whose 'Goodnight Ladies' triumphed
O'er all but Spring's most blustery gales
Choirs which daily met to practise
For the Music Competition
For the day which showed New Talents
The day of Trenance Rugby Songs!
In the Summer sunshine last week
In Luxulyan's Church's Choir Stalls,
We enjoyed Fowey Brass Band's Music,
And sang 'Zadoc's' well known anthem,
Performed some lesser known Easter songs.
So to end this year of music
Of players and of singers joining
Joining in the music making
We'll put on our annual concert
And we hope that you will join us
Friends and parents come to listen.'

Dramatic activities were largely concentrated in the annual School Play. Mr Farnham-Flower reigned supreme with assistance from various members of staff, especially Mr Lincoln. In 1964 it was decided to have two casts, the A and the B. This would allow twice as many pupils to perform and would also overcome the problem of sickness, accident or even university interview. Thus Anouilh's *The Lark* began a trend which was to continue through *Pygmalian, A Midsummer Night's Dream, An Italian Straw Hat*, the challenging double bill of Ionesco's *The Bald Primadonna* and, with the music department, Britten's *Noyes Fludde*, to *Arms and the Man* with a B cast giv-

A Midſommer nights dreame.

Written by William Shakeſpeare.

Programme of the School Production 1967

ing performances on alternate nights. The Play always involved vast armies of people besides the casts, doing such essential, but unseen work, as back stage, selling tickets and programmes, car parking and so on. It always was a real event in the School calendar. This rubbed off on the rest of the School and in 1967 a Junior Drama Group began and produced two plays, Obey's *Noah* and Barwis' *Captain Swing*. A new but successful venture came in March 1973, when Richard Turner, an Old Boy but now a member of the English staff, produced *Under Milk Wood* with a mixed cast of staff and VIth Form. This format was to continue into the Sixth Form College. As with music there was a House Speech Competition, organised in a similar way to the Music Competition. Choirs were trained in collective rendering of poems, scenes usually from Shakespeare were enacted and individuals delivered a speech on a chosen subject – one year, one Kenneth Martin (1959-66) gave an impassioned account of how he would organise the Cornish to repel the English from a stronghold around St Dennis church, using broccoli as ammunition! Rivalry was keen. 'The House Speech Competition comes but once a year – and for that we are truly thankful. I don't think our nerves, tempers or tonsils would be able to stand more' wrote Helen Goldsworthy in 1966. Nevertheless unexpected talent was unearthed and interest stimulated.

The House system was brought in line with the Boys' School who had already introduced a fourth House. In 1962, Tregrehan was added, with appropriate adjustment for the girls, making each House reasonably manageable. Points were accumulated as before from competitions in sport, music and speech; the stars and stripes arrangements also contributed or removed points.

According to the memories of old students much of the day to day discipline was carried out by prefects. Roger Fogg (1960-5) recounts how they were generally made to stand in the corridor or do lines. On one occasion when some dastardly deed had been done 'one of the principal detectives in the case was John Nettles, rehearsing for his forthcoming Bergerac series'.

Societies proliferated, and waxed and waned according to the energy and enthusiasm of the VIth Form members who were significant in helping the staff generate interest. In 1963-4 the Philosophical Society enjoyed a programme of wide interest from book reviews, debates, a brains trust, and an address by Mormon Missionaries to an account of life in a prisoner of war camp. It continued to have a similar eclectic programme and in early 1966, national events prompted the holding of a mock election which enlivened things and was won by the Liberals. By 1970 its activities were largely but not exclusively debating, on such issues as war ethics (hawks won), female emancipation (emancipators lost) and the existence of free will (split vote). Members of the Scientific Society were introduced, in 1963, to Tel-Star and the use of satellite stations for communications, including a visit to Goonhilly to see it in operation. There were expeditions to the Marine Biology Laboratory in Plymouth and a lecture by Dr Clark of the ECC Laboratories on the *Science of China Clay* as well as regular films on scientific matters. 1965 saw an impressive programme which included *Stereophonic Sound* and *The Electronic Computer*. That year, too, saw the beginning of the Junior branch, but it seems to have been rather short-lived. By choosing a local 'celebrity' as president each year, useful contacts were made; 1970-71 was particularly good when Dr Dennison of ECLP proved to be very helpful. One disappointment was in 1970 when the Nancekuke Biochemical Research establishment was not able to provide a lecturer. The SCM (Student Christian Movement) put in a brief appearance in 1963-4 and reappeared as the Scripture Union in 1970, with joint meetings with Bodmin Grammar School's Christian Group. The Photographic Club was to have a much greater and longer lasting appeal with its emphasis on equipment and techniques. The Readers and Writers Club bemoaned the lack of response from the body of the school and in 1967 was looking for a new vitality from the middle school in particular. Clearly this was forthcoming as it was still going fairly strongly in 1971. By the late 1960s a Chess Club was beginning to make its name. It was able to enter the Grenville Cup competition claiming a few notable scalps. In 1969 David Jonas and Stephen Patterson were selected for the Cornwall Junior Chess Team. 1965 saw the formation of an Historical Society, coinciding with the School's membership of the Historical Association which usually held its meetings in Truro. Most of its activity was attending lectures by eminent his-

CHOW 1972. Barry Farley with his class from London, with various attendant VIth formers

torians on a variety of topics although there was an entertaining, but damp, visit to the Minack Theatre for *1066 And All That* performed by Southampton University.

In 1969 a Social Activities Group was formed in order to support local charities as much as possible, either by providing physical help or by raising money. One member spent two mornings a week during the summer holidays, helping at the St Austell Play Group and several 'manned' stalls at East Cornwall Society for the Mentally Handicapped Summer Fair. A Lower VI former did gardening for Miss Parry who lived in Tregonissey Road and others helped at St Lawrence's Old People's Christmas Party at the Church Hall. The main thrust of the group was to raise money and support CHOW (Cornish Holidays on Wheels). This had been formed in 1969, by various local organisations, prompted by TocH and including amongst others, St Austell Scouts, ECLP, Barclays Bank and the School. Two members of the Lower VI, Susan Greaves and Pauline Blacker, were very interested in helping others in some way and per-

suaded me to go with them to the inaugural meeting. From that developed a group which was to last throughout the years of the Sixth Form College, until 1992. During the first year they raised the then considerable sum of £700 from a variety of activities. The most fruitful of these was a sponsored walk which raised £428, and others included Coffee Mornings, a Top Team competition based on 'It's a Knock-out', a Christmas Bazaar and carol singing. With support from other local establishments including West Hill Secondary School's special performance of *Sweeney Todd*, CHOW was able, in 1971, to entertain the first group of children from London to spend a week's holiday in Cornwall – a holiday they would not have had otherwise. They came with their teacher, Angela Yelland, herself an Old Girl of the School (1959-66) and caravans were hired and parked outside the Sixth Form Centre. The children slept in the caravans while a body of students slept in the Centre where they cooked for the group. During the day, the children were taken on outings, such as swimming in the sea (a novelty), boat trips with

Mr Thomas from Fowey, visits to local places such as Flambards and farms, and just playing in and walking around the grounds. The following year Barry Farley, an Old Boy, brought his class from another London primary school. In 1973, Deborah Dickinson (1972-5) and her friends decided to produce a student pantomime to swell the funds. The first student written and produced performance was *Cinderella* and included as many non-drama students as possible, especially from the football team. One performance was given to the students of Blantyre Training Centre. Thus began another successful tradition which was to last through the Sixth Form College until the early 1990s. While the pantomime was an annual affair another innovation *The Frolics* was rather more spasmodic. This was a staff/student review and threw up some likely, and unlikely talent!

The School Scout Group enjoyed positive support from Mr Brinkworth and between 1957 and 1967 produced eleven Queen Scouts. In 1963 the Senior Scouts embarked on a two week trip, in a Dormobile, through France and Spain with Mr Cooper during the Easter holidays. A long trek through France, by way of Rouen and Chartres, resulted in the crossing of the Pyrenees to Pamplona and, eventually three days in Barcelona, before starting back again. In July 1966 the troop played host to an American Eagle Scout and his Scout Leader father, leading to useful exchange of ideas and practices. The starting of a Cub Scout Pack in 1966 added to the problems already encountered by the Scouts of finding suitable accommodation for meetings. Demands on use of the Hall at the end of the School day and in the early evening, led to more desire for a separate Scout HQ. However the group continued to flourish with P Mitchell and M Zimber being the first in the area to achieve the new Chief Scout Award in 1968. By 1971 when Carl Roberts, an Old Boy and an 'old scout', stood down as Group Scout Leader, there were 65 members of the group, enjoying such activities as canoeing as well as various camping episodes. It is alleged that they beat the record, quoted in the Guinness Book of Records, by tying 96,416 knots in a sponsored knot tying marathon, raising £120 for their funds!

The Girl Guide Company celebrated its 21st birthday in 1963 and its programme changed very little. There was always the urgency to prepare 1st formers for their Tenderfoot, ready for enrolment just before Christmas by Miss Husband. Established guides worked away at gaining their badges as well as undertaking various fund raising activities. They always supported the National Children's Homes raising about £12 each year with a senior Guide attending the service in St John's when contributions were made. In 1966 they helped at a fete at Blantyre to raise money for a minibus to transport handicapped children. Social activity was not neglected. Each autumn parents were invited to view the work of the patrols, to sample some cooking and, usually, to watch a playlet. Pam Whitney (Harper 1962-7) says "Apart from the Halloween Parties we held, I remember a group of us putting on a play, *The Reluctant Dragon*. By the time we had made the costume for the dragon, learnt our lines etc, we were referring to the play as *The Reluctant Drag On!*" It was also memorable for the splendid dragon's head made by Mrs Steward of the Art Department. Then in the summer there was always a day's outing, usually to a place of historic interest. In 1963 Miss Newton joined the staff as a Mathematics teacher and she gave great support at the weekly meetings, and in 1965, Miss Smart, who was a student for a term, also gave valuable assistance in helping to produce a play. By 1969 it was felt that the Company based on the School had out lived its real purpose as there were, now, so many more opportunities for girls to socialise in their home communities than there had been during the War. So it was disbanded and a Girls' Adventure and Science Society (GAS) took its place, but this did not last long either.

An innovation in the 1960s was the Sixth Form Conferences organised by County Hall. They began in 1962 and each March schools were invited to send a number of VIth formers to the Kilbirnie Hotel in Newquay, over a weekend. Staff were also required to attend, for disciplinary reasons as well as educational, and by 1967, eight pupils from St Austell were part of the 200 participants. The themes ranged from *Human Relations* in 1963, through *Communications* to *The Age of Explosion* in 1967 and *University Education and its Future* in 1969. The programme was one of lectures, discussion groups and question sessions to the eminent speakers. Those who attended

2nd St Austell Guide Company as part of the procession to celebrate Commonwealth Sunday 1963

appreciated the opportunity to meet with a different group of their peers, as well as the excellent food provided!

The arrival of Mr Courtney Rice in the Geography Department in 1962 led to annual field work trips. They began, in a rather modest way, at Easter 1967, when Mr John Batey took sixteen VIth formers to Swanage in Dorset for a two day inspection of the geographical features of the coast line. At Lulworth Cove they were thrilled, to see in reality one of the illustrations in every text book of physical geography. This was a joint expedition with Newton Abbot Grammar School – a blow to the sixteen who thought they had the 40 seater coach to themselves. From that beginning came the annual expeditions to South Wales. In 1968, 30 VIth formers under the guidance of Mr Rice and three members of staff spent a week at 'Coleg y Fro', a YMCA near Cardiff during which they surveyed the Gower peninsula, carried out a transect of the Rhondda Valley, attempted to climb a Brecon Beacon, visited the new town, Cwmbran, and the boys went down a coal mine

– a feature out of bounds to females. One result of the latter activity was that the boys became amazingly attractive as the coal dust which was very difficult to remove from around the eyes, resembled mascara! Steven Pinch's summary that 'we learned a great deal and our enthusiasm for the subject was greatly increased' was no doubt echoed by following years.

Other departments, too, organised curriculum related excursions but only as day trips, such as the Lower VI visit to King Edward Mine at the Camborne School of Mines in 1963. St Austell Brewery and Goonhilly Downs followed as did the biologists' outings to the Plymouth Aquarium and, in April 1970, a tour of the Science Laboratories at Exeter University. Dr Wilson, Mr Wolstenholme and their successors took the VIth Form scientists to the Christmas Lecture by the Royal Institute of Chemists each year in Plymouth. These outings were not confined to the senior school as in July 1966, all the Ist Form went to the Minack Theatre to see *Toad of Toad Hall*, in February 1970 the IVth Form saw *As You Like It* in Truro by the Northcott Players and in July 1970 and 1971 the History Department took the first year to Restormel Castle.

As the School was so much larger outside speakers were invited only to address sections of the school community. Many of these talks were to the Vth or VIth Forms concerning career opportunities in certain fields, such as *Nursing as a Career* in 1963, representatives from ECLP describing opportunities available to Vth Form leavers in 1968 and, successively, lecturers from different universities suggesting options at their establishments. In the early 1960s there continued to be talks such as *Malaysia* to the IIIrd Forms, Lt. Ellis of the Royal Navy on *Scott of the Antarctic*, a Commonwealth lecture on *East Africa* to the IInd Forms, a talk to the Lower VI, in April 1971, on the work at the Pestalozzi Village and, in November 1971, the return of an Old Boy, James Hodge, a distinguished physicist and an expert on steam engines, spoke on *Trevithick*. These gradually ceased and it was the individual societies, such as the Scientific Society, which entertained specialists in their own fields.

Speech Days, too, which lasted until 1969, provided another occasion when eminent people were invited to present prizes and make appropriate speeches. These days had become massive affairs with the whole School being 'marched' through the town to the 'old' Odeon Cinema, the only building capable of holding everyone. The walk through the town is remembered by many pupils including Peter Swain (1966-73), and Susan Hart (Hooper 1963-69) who considers that 'it was quite an impressive sight'. Juliet Rees (Wallis 1962-8) remembers Speech Day for a different reason. As Head Girl, together with the Head Boy, she had to make a speech during the proceedings. 'The Grammar School was about 800 pupils, plus staff and parents and I was very nervous, but as I am very short-sighted and, at that time, too vain to wear my glasses, all I could see was a blur!'

Careers education and preparation for 'life after school' gained much greater prominence. The autumn of 1971 saw an evening of mock interviews when six 'volunteers' from the Upper VI were interviewed by a panel representing the main career paths – the pupils' performances were discussed afterwards. This was repeated the following year when parents, too, were invited. In July

1973 a careers forum was held for the VIth Form. Speakers covered a range of options. The main focus was university, training college and polytechnic, but representatives from Social Services, the Hospital Services, ECLP, the Police Force and the W/RAF broadened the scope. The next day all the new Vth formers were given careers talks by representatives from the County Careers Service.

Parents' Evenings became an increasingly prominent feature in the School calendar. The first record we have is in May 1965 when parents of Vth and VIth formers met with the staff in the Hall and the following year parents of the Vth formers were invited to meet staff to consider options in the VIth Form. In July of that year parents of the IIIrd Form also met with members of staff to discuss O Level options. Mr Wolstenholme who succeeded Mr Martin as Senior Master, prided himself on being able to construct a timetable around whatever choices a pupil made. These meetings then were held each year with encouraging attendance. In September, 1967 parents of new Ist formers were invited to see the School and meet the staff followed by IInd year parents in November and by the beginning of 1968 parents of every year were invited to the School at appropriate times in the School year. In 1968 a Parent Teacher Association (PTA) was formed and, besides social evenings, staff were invited to speak to parents on issues deemed to be of interest – for instance, the work of certain departments or School journeys.

What did expand considerably was the number of excursions both out of the county and out of the country. A party went to Stratford-upon-Avon and Coventry at half term 1962 and in June 1966, 88 members of the IIIrd Form were accompanied to the Royal Cornwall Show by Mr Crabb and Mrs Yelland. Spring 1969 saw a party of IIIrd and IVth formers spending three days in London when diverse activities included St Paul's Cathedral, Petticoat Lane, a visit to the BBC and 'a bitterly cold boat trip to Greenwich'. A similar trip was repeated at Easter 1971 with similar personnel, Mrs Sales, Mr Cooper and Mr and Mrs John Mitchell, and included a visit to the Ford Motor Company at Dagenham. In 1963, Miss Mary Ingram started taking small groups of A Level German students to Cambridge University, one of the very few places in England where it was

THE EDUCATIONAL CRUISE   Hazel Duddy, U.II.A.

'The Educational Cruise' by Hazel Duddy from the School Magazine 1964-5

possible to see productions by certain Colleges, of plays in German. In 1972 Mrs Sales took a small party to Northumberland and on another History excursion to London, in the spring half term of 1974, I took eleven VIth formers for a 'cultural' weekend which included a visit to Hampton Court and a vegetarian meal in an early specialised vegetarian restaurant – the latter, an experience not universally appreciated!

Further afield, in August, 1963, Mr Rice and a stalwart band of staff took a party of 42 VIth formers on a long train journey to Switzerland. They stayed at Weggis for a week enjoying the spectacular scenery, sometimes on foot. The cost was £33. In April 1966 a party went with Miss Bridgewater, Mr Lincoln, Mr Mervyn Thomas and Mrs Truscott to northern France, including three days in Paris where they stayed in an hotel with six flights of stairs ensuring that the hotel lift, 'a sort of elaborate bird cage', was in almost constant use. At the same time a small group braved a week of snow and freezing north German weather in Lubeck with Miss Ingram and Mr Gardner where they enjoyed aspects of the culture as well as practising their German. They were particularly impressed at being able to understand the sermon when attending a church service!

This was the era of the educational cruise when LEAs could take up a number of places on SS Uganda for journeys to far flung places in the Mediterranean. The first was in the autumn of 1964. The participants, from the Vth and VIth Forms, were flown to Venice where they joined the ship and travelled to Sardinia, Athens, Tangiers and Lisbon. Days at sea involved compulsory lessons and some voluntary activities. Angela Hurst (Yelland 1959-66) wrote in the Magazine: 'I decided to attend Italian lessons and learn some useful phrases. This I did, but unfortunately we had left Italy by the time I was ready to use them!' Days in port were spent either visiting the city or, as at Tangiers, with a coach tour through the countryside, where, as Jean Wearing (1958-65) recounted: 'some of the more intrepid members had rides on grumpy camels'. They were held every two years but we did not participate in 1967. This could have been because Mr Brinkworth had complained about their taking a fortnight of the School year, inevitably at a busy time. The second cruise, in October 1969, left from Falmouth and travelled for two days to Cueta in Spanish North Africa from where they visited the Moroccan town of Tetouan. Corsica, and Napoleon, was the next port of call before docking in Leghorn which enabled the vast company to visit Florence and Pisa by coach. Then it was past Gibraltar to Lisbon before the last lap home to Falmouth. On the third, in 1971, the two weeks included Gibraltar, Lisbon, Algiers and Vigo. There was much to be learned on these ventures not only about new countries and new cultures but also about living communally – many did not find it easy to sleep in a dormitory with 27 others. They were truly educational cruises.

Easter 1969 saw 39 IInd Form pupils on a week's Rhine cruise, organised by Mr Lincoln, which included a rough Channel crossing from Ostend but a much calmer cruise. The best the Rhine valley could offer including Cologne was explored – 'It's a Gothic Cathedral; a religion not alive in England', one young person wrote. There was cultural exchange – overheard in a Rudesheim Souvenir Shop: 'I've bought a cow-bell for my Mum'. At Easter 1970, with Mr Mervyn Thomas and Mr and Mrs John Mitchell, I embarked on the first of a series of VIth Form visits to Florence. We stayed in Florence for ten days and packed in as many of the wonders of that city as possible. There were also excursions to Fiesole by service bus and Siena and San Gimignano by coach for a full day. On our return we entertained parents to displays of the experience, with Italian fare of spaghetti and chianti, hopefully assuring the parents that their money had been well spent. These trips were to continue every other year throughout the 1970s. In 1970 Mr Ken Hunter and Mr Robinson took a party to the Commonwealth Games in Edinburgh while Mr Wearing embarked on an exchange visit to Morlaix in France with members of the IVth Forms in June 1971, their counterparts joining the School on their return. This, too, became a regular feature of the School calendar. In March 1972 a group of junior and middle school pupils visited Paris with Mr Keith Watson and Miss Sonia Rowe, and some members of the IVth Form took part in a German exchange. Thus, during these years a significant number of pupils had the opportunity of European travel and a significant number of staff gave up some of their holiday to make it possible. On the whole, the staff enjoyed

The first group to visit Florence in the Spring of 1970, waiting on Florence station for the train home

the experiences as much as the pupils!

Individual pupils, too, spread their wings and spent varying periods in Europe. In 1966 Duncan McGaw spent two weeks in Cologne and Bonn, Marilyn and Kathryn Clymo spent three months in Stuttgart and Munich, practising their German and performing various household tasks for their hosts, and Belinda Truscott was in France for nine months, most of which was spent in Bordeaux and its surroundings, again, soaking up the culture and perfecting her French.

The winter weather in the 1960s and early '70s was more severe than it is now. During the long, cold winter of 1962/3 the frost was so intense that it froze all the lavatories and the School was closed for two days. This, too, has featured largely in memories! In February, 1969, after a snow fall, there were forecasts of blizzards and the School was sent home at midday – the blizzard did come, but not until after midnight! Again in February 1973 snow forced the cancellation of a Parents' Evening as well as the sending home of everyone at lunch time. During the winter of 1971/2, the

so called 'Winter of Discontent' when the miners' strike resulted in widespread power cuts, the student pantomime was in danger of falling at the first hurdle, but the audience was asked to bring torches which, mercifully, were not required! Supplies of fuel ran out in February and all but the Vth and VIth Forms were sent home, hopefully to find warmth there, while the examination forms had to cope as well as possible. The power situation also led to the cancellation of the VIth Form Parents' Evening on March 1st.

School children, and staff, at this time still were able to benefit from events deemed to be of national, or at least significant local interest. In July 1966, Cornish schools had a day's holiday when the Queen came to open the new County Hall and, again, in June 1970 when the Prince of Wales visited the Royal Cornwall Show. In November 1972, all schools were closed for the Queen's Silver Wedding celebrations. Clearly those were more indulgent days, but I do not remember a day's holiday when we won the World Cup – perhaps we thought it would not be a one-off!

Christmas helped to make the School buildings look festive with decorations in form rooms. The VIth Form helped to organise parties for years I and II which took place during the last week of term and were accompanied by much noisy merrymaking.

Remembrance Day services were held each year as near to November 11th as possible. There was a short service in the Hall for the senior school, followed by a shorter one on the stairs by the memorial window and the board with the names of the 39 Old Boys who had been killed.

On the staff the 'old order' was changing. Mr Martin, who was beyond normal retirement age, was given permission to continue in order to help to see the new School established. He retired in the summer of 1965 after 41 years of service in the School in both of its mixed eras, as well as in the entire life of the Boys' School. Besides teaching History to generations of boys, and rather fewer girls, he was also Senior Master for his last three years and a sportsman of note, particularly on the cricket pitch and as an administrator of County Football after he stopped playing. As Squadron Leader of the ATC for more than twenty years he played his part in training young men for the RAF during the War, and continuing basic 'air-mindedness' training after it. At the time his son, Laurence, was the only Old Austellian to have become a University Professor. A pupil's assessment was; 'Mr Martin strikes me as a local landmark'.

Two years later, Mr Brinkworth, already a sick man, himself retired. He gave 23 years of service to St Austell, first at the Boys' School and then guiding the Mixed School through a potentially difficult transition period. He was determined that each establishment should sustain high standards of behaviour, work and English grammar and punctuation. There was a strict dress code for staff and Alan Hutt remembers being gently reprimanded for wearing a sports coat and I have never forgotten how to spell 'exuberant', having spelt it incorrectly on a report. His plan for the pastoral arrangements in the new School, not only divided it into manageable groups but also ensured that the rump of the Girls' School staff was given a real stake in the administration, as most Heads of Department were men, the women having left. He was dedicated to fostering the culture both of the School and the community. He was one of the founding members of the St Austell Arts Club having a particular interest in music and poetry. He introduced Music Appreciation to the Boys' curriculum and his innovative annual Rededication Service reflected his deeply held Christian views and was a regular feature of school life until 1968. Ist former comments in the Magazine of 1967 say 'He even taught my Dad. I think he deserves a break after all that', 'He is very well mannered – quite a gentleman'.

Sadly Mr Brinkworth was not to enjoy a long retirement and he died in March 1968. His funeral was at the Parish Church and was attended by most of the staff and the School Choir. This was not an easy time as in December 1967, Sylvia Crowle, who had been Head Girl 1964/5, was killed in a car crash on her way home for Christmas from Westminster Training College. After a public as well as School subscription, a memorial bust was commissioned which is now in St Austell College. Three years later, in December 1970, Philip Parker, too, was killed in a road accident in Oxford. He had left in the summer and was a student at Wadham College. These were just two of the pupils and recent ex-pupils who died, most of them as the result of accidents

Mr Rex Thomas succeeded Mr Brinkworth as Headmaster and this began a series of huge changes. He had been Headmaster of Fowey Grammar School and, on his leaving, that school closed and amalgamated with the Secondary Modern becoming Fowey Comprehensive. He brought his VIth Form to St Austell and, together with those coming from Penrice and West Hill Secondary Schools, the VIth Form swelled to 221 by 1971. In the summer term, 1969, the Sixth Form Centre, at the far west of the buildings, was opened and a Sixth Form Council elected to help to manage its affairs. The two teaching rooms and the common room with a coffee/snack bar, together with usual 'facilities' was to be the centre of VIth Form activity, certainly a new concept in the life of the School. Dr Wilson, who retired in 1969 after 23 years of teaching in St Austell, gave two teak benches to enhance the outside of the building and provide a place of rest for weary VIth formers. Under the guidance of Alan Hutt the Council ran the bar, generally to the satisfaction of all, although Kathy Jones (Stevens 1962-9) remembers that on

The Sixth Form Centre opened in 1969. It was not the most beautiful building but it served its purpose

one occasion 'the hot drink dispenser dispensed ants in the beverage powders', and they organised what were called 'socials' but were in fact discos. There were difficulties here as those who were not members of the VIth Form came and, sometimes, caused trouble. In 1972 it was decreed that they would be open only to present and old students. Inevitably there were complaints about the building – it was too small, the revolutionary heating system did not really heat, the Council would impose martial law – but it did work. The VIth Form was welded into a unit and it was a foretaste, as well as a trial period for things to come.

In July 1971, there began the tradition of inviting new members of the VIth Form for a two week introductory course when they would sample A Level courses to help them make decisions for September. Besides those from local secondary schools, pupils from further afield came, particularly from Tregony and Wadebridge as well as a few from the Isles of Scilly. There were also a few really foreign students – an American scholar came for a year in 1968 and Horatio, a student from Botswana, joined us in 1970.

In response to the government Circular 10/65, requesting that Local Education Authorities proceed with plans to introduce comprehensive education, as early as October 1966, a Working Party of the County Education Committee had met to consider the reorganisation of secondary educa-

tion in the St Austell district. Its draft proposals of a new Sixth Form College, on the site earmarked for a new Grammar School building at Wheal Eliza, fed by four comprehensives was accepted in principle and supported by the local head teachers and staff representatives. The appointment of Mr Thomas saw the movement towards the new structure gather pace. In the Spring term of 1970 he gained a Schoolmaster Fellowship at Oxford University to investigate further the formation and management of Sixth Form Colleges, while Miss Husband ran the School as acting head. At the same time, the LEA put forward its programme of major building for 1971/2. A Sixth Form College for some 400 students, together with extensions to Fowey and Penrice to enhance their buildings for comprehensive education was estimated to cost £609,537 with a further £64,700 was to be spent on St Stephens and the Grammar School buildings – a technical block was already being built for Poltair on the tennis courts of the old Girls' School. This caused some sadness as a lovely white rambling rose around the hard court, remembered by Sue Sharland (Burton 1955-62), disappeared and she says 'I particularly remember a beautiful old oak tree which was subsequently cut down to make way for the technical block.' Around this tree there had been a bench placed there in memory of a girl who had died while a pupil in the Girls' School, by her parents. Plans for a Sports complex, in conjunction with the local authorities of St Austell and Fowey in the grounds of the Grammar School did not materialise.

In September, 1971 the Grammar School started a new year without a Ist Form entry and in 1972 the Grammar School, now considerably reduced in numbers, shared its buildings with West Hill Secondary School, now known as Poltair Comprehensive. The LEA guaranteed employment for all staff and some left to take up positions in the new comprehensives. Mr Thomas was to be Principal of the new Sixth Form College and Miss Husband, Vice-Principal. The rump of the Grammar School moved westwards towards the Brewery while Poltair moved in from the east. By 1973 some of the accommodation of the new Sixth Form College, built on the St Austell Cricket Ground not at Wheal Eliza, was ready and the evacuation of the Grammar School buildings began in earnest. That year the LEA decreed that the establishment should be called 'The Grammar School and Sixth Form College' and in June 1975, when the last entry had gone through, the Grammar School finally ceased to exist after 67 years.

Generations of Cornish children had passed through its doors. While for some the experience was not an unqualified success, for many, certainly of those who have contributed to this exercise, it was a very positive experience both academically as well as personally. Jenny Rudge (Shortall 1964-71) maybe speaks for many when she says 'They were great days. It was a great privilege to go St Austell Grammar School, to be Head Girl and to be offered 2 Es by the university of my choice to read History. I took the path of testing my leadership faculty rather than academic ability; it was a fantastic foundation. They say it is largely about the feeling of life rather than the meaning of life. Well, it felt good.'

The Vth Forms of the Grammar School in 1974-5 just before the buildings were finally vacated

APPENDICES

I. Headteachers/Deputies
Mixed School 1908-33
Headteacher
1908-10 Mr WD Raynor
1910-21 Mr A Jenkinson
(1915-19 Mr Lodge)
1921-33 Mr WV Barritt

Deputy
1908-Dec 1913 Miss M Passmore
Jan 1914-16 Miss E Lomas
1916-18 Miss L Twigg
1919-21 Miss M Griffiths
1921-33 Miss A Bond

Boys' School 1933-62
Headmaster
1933-44 Mr Barritt
1944-62 Mr GH Brinkworth

Deputy
1933-44 Mr Lodge
1944-62 Mr T Richardson

Girls' School 1933-62
Headmistress
1933-50 Miss Bond
1950-62 Miss FLE Camous

Deputy
1933-50 Miss R Lewis
1950-57 Mrs Goode
1957-62 Miss M Husband

Mixed School 1962-75
Headmaster
1962-7 Mr GH Brinkworth
1967-75 Mr RH Thomas

Deputy
1962-75 Miss M Husband

Senior Master
1962-5 Mr L Martin
1965-71 Mr J Wolstenholme
1971-5 Mr J Wearing

II. The boys who died in the two World Wars
1914-18
Arthur Cyril Bennett
William Thomas Morton
Reginald Montague Coon
Sydney Pearce
William James Lawry
John Carhart Reed
William Merrifield
Sydney Herbert Rundle
William Nancarrow
1939-45
Arthur John Ash
Stanley Perry Lodge
Joseph Peter Bassett
Leonard Lobb
Peter John Bradfield
James Gilholme Moore
Leonard Redvers Bray
William Ray Moyse
Archibald William Burt
Ross Odgers
Richard George Woodley Crossman
Eric Phillimore Bassett Organ
Clifford Austen Crowle
Sidney Frederick Pascoe
William Kenneth Dunn
Jack Passmore
John Christopher Gribble
Evan Gilbert Pugh
Osborne John Hilton Hawke
Douglas Reynolds
John Henry Hibbert
William Henry Sturtridge
Eric Claude Hooper
Roy Trahair
Percy Keast
Charles Edward Truscott
Gordon Edward Kendall
John Wiseman
Reginald John Kernick
Jack Yelland

III. Red River Valley
It's a long time now I've been waiting
For the words that you never did say
And it's now that my fond heart is breaking
For they say you are going away.

Then linger awhile ere you leave us
Do not hasten to bid us adieu
But remember the Red River Valley
And the maiden who loved you so true.

And should you ever return
To this lone prairie land of the west
May the white girl you marry remember
That the red maiden loved you the best.

This rather inappropriate song will be remembered by former pupils of the Girls' Grammar School, of a certain vintage, as well as staff. It is still sung, with great enthusiasm, at many a reunion.